Fresh Ways with
Patisserie

COVER
Sugar-frosted rose and freesia petals decorate miniature ring cakes filled with a kirsch-flavoured cream (recipe, page 70). A sparing quantity of cream, whipped to increase its bulk and lightened with stiffly beaten egg white, provides a luxurious filling without overburdening the calorie count.

TIME-LIFE BOOKS

EUROPEAN EDITOR: Ellen Phillips
Design Director: Ed Skyner
Director of Editorial Resources: Louise Tulip
Chief Sub-Editor: Ilse Gray

LOST CIVILIZATIONS
HOW THINGS WORK
SYSTEM EARTH
LIBRARY OF CURIOUS AND
UNUSUAL FACTS
BUILDING BLOCKS
A CHILD'S FIRST LIBRARY OF LEARNING
VOYAGE THROUGH THE UNIVERSE
THE THIRD REICH
MYSTERIES OF THE UNKNOWN
TIME-LIFE HISTORY OF THE WORLD
FITNESS, HEALTH & NUTRITION
HEALTHY HOME COOKING
UNDERSTANDING COMPUTERS
THE ENCHANTED WORLD
LIBRARY OF NATIONS
PLANET EARTH
THE GOOD COOK
THE WORLD'S WILD PLACES

ISBN 0 7054 2008 6
TIME-LIFE is a trademark of Time Warner Inc. U.S.A.

HEALTHY HOME COOKING

SERIES DIRECTOR: Jackie Matthews
Studio Stylist: Liz Hodgson
Editorial Assistant: Eugénie Romer

Editorial Staff for *Fresh Ways with Patisserie:*
Editor: Frances Dixon
Researcher: Ellen Dupont
Designer: Paul Reeves
Sub-Editor: Christine Noble

PICTURE DEPARTMENT
Administrator: Patricia Murray
Picture Co-ordinator: Amanda Hindley

EDITORIAL PRODUCTION
Chief: Maureen Kelly
Assistant: Samantha Hill
Editorial Department: Theresa John, Debra Lelliott

THE CONTRIBUTORS

JOANNA BLYTHMAN is a cook and recipe writer who owns a specialist food shop in Edinburgh. She contributes articles on cookery to a number of newspapers and trade periodicals.

SILVIJA DAVIDSON studied at Leith's School of Food and Wine and specializes in the development of recipes from Latvia and other international cuisines.

JANICE MURFITT trained as a home economist and worked as a cookery editor on *Family Circle* magazine. Her primary interest now is developing recipes for cakes and pastries; her titles include *Cake Icing and Decorating* and *Cheesecakes and Flans.*

HILARY WALDEN is a trained food technologist and experienced cookery writer. In addition to contributing to the major cookery journals she has also written many books, including *Home Baking* and *The Book of French Patisserie.*

The following also contributed recipes to this volume: Maddalena Bonino, Joanna Farrow, Yvonne Hamlett, Carole Handslip, Rosemary Wadey, Lorna Walker, Jeni Wright.

THE COOKS

The recipes in this book were cooked for photography by Pat Alburey, Jacki Baxter, Jill Eggleton, Joanna Farrow, Anne Gains, Carole Handslip, Dolly Meers, Janice Murfitt, Jane Suthering, Rosemary Wadey. *Studio Assistant:* Rita Walters.

CONSULTANT

PAT ALBUREY is a home economist with a wide experience of preparing foods for photography, teaching cookery and creating recipes. She has written a number of cookery books including *The Harrods Book of Cakes and Desserts,* and she was the studio consultant for the Time-Life series *The Good Cook.* In addition to acting as the general consultant on this volume, she also created a number of the recipes.

NUTRITION CONSULTANT

PATRICIA JUDD trained as a dietician and worked in hospital practice before returning to university to obtain her MSc and PhD degrees. Since then she has lectured in Nutrition and Dietetics at London University.

Nutritional analyses for *Fresh Ways with Patisserie* were derived from McCance and Widdowson's *The Composition of Food* by A. A. Paul and D. A. T. Southgate, and other current data.

This volume is one of a series of illustrated cookery books that emphasize the preparation of healthy dishes for today's weight-conscious, nutrition-minded eaters.

Fresh Ways with Patisserie

BY

THE EDITORS OF TIME-LIFE BOOKS

TIME-LIFE BOOKS/AMSTERDAM

Contents

Quince and Chestnut Strudel

Caramel-Topped Apple Choux Fingers

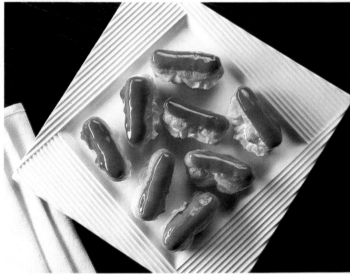

A Trio of Meringues

3 Delicate Confections 103

Spicy Pear Roulade

Maple Sweetmeats

4 Patisserie from the Microwave 129

The New Patisserie

As ravishing to the eye as it is delicious, patisserie is the most bewitching branch of the culinary art. The simplest of ingredients — flour, sugar, butter, eggs and cream — are transformed by the cook's alchemy into flaky short-crust, tender choux, feather-light sponge and melting meringue, temptingly embellished with chocolate, nuts, fruit and icing. The names of these confections are as beguiling as their appearance; souffléed coffee diamonds *(page 33)*, poppy seed pillows *(page 54)* and chocolate kisses *(page 107)* are just some of the 120 recipes that have been devised and selected for this volume.

Of course no one eats such frivolities out of necessity; they are an indulgence, and so might seem to merit exclusion from a healthy diet. Fortunately, so harsh a regime is not necessary. By paring down the amounts of fat, cholesterol and sugar, patisserie can still be enjoyed in moderation. In fact there is no reason why a 2,000-calorie daily diet should not include both a pastry dessert and a sweet baked snack, provided fat and sugar levels in the rest of the day's meals are limited, since most of the recipes on the following pages contain less than 250 calories per portion.

Many of the featured recipes are entirely new creations that satisfy the modern taste for lighter, healthier food. Also included are versions of traditional French classics — meringue whirls, chocolate éclairs, iced petits fours and other culinary gems that rank among the glories of the *pâtissier's* art. The special challenge of this volume has been to adapt these favourites to sensible dietary requirements, because traditionally it is the flavour and moistness of butter, the velvety smoothness of egg yolks, the richness of whipped cream and the sweetness of sugar that contribute so much to their appeal.

Devising the new patisserie

The challenge has been met in a combination of ways: by judiciously reducing the quantities of ingredients such as sugar

and egg yolk, by substituting them with others that perform the same purpose, and by using a light hand with fillings and any final embellishments. These methods, devised and tested in the Healthy Home Cooking kitchens, produce results that lack nothing in their flavour, texture or appearance.

Sugar has been kept to a minimum by reducing, where possible, the quantity used in the basic doughs and batters, and by avoiding thick, sticky icings and cloying fillings. Since sweetness is the essence of patisserie, however, and sugar is an indispensable structural element of meringues and other confections, it is seldom entirely omitted from a recipe.

Weight for weight, fats contribute about twice as many calories as sugar, so they too are included only in sufficient quantities to produce the desired result. Whereas most recipes using phyllo pastry call for a generous coating of butter between each layer, the recipes in this volume use the merest film to achieve the same effect. Cream is used sparingly but seductively. Where whipped cream is called for, the amount can be reduced by blending it with low-calorie beaten egg whites — as in the recipe for petal ring cakes on page 70. For some recipes *fromage frais* or yogurt make excellent substitutes for cream.

When using fat, the amount is not the only important consideration; the type of fat used is probably just as crucial. The choice lies between the polyunsaturated fats, which are exclusively of vegetable origin, and the saturated fats such as butter, which come mainly from animal sources. Saturated fats raise the level of blood cholesterol, and a high level of blood cholesterol is implicated in coronary heart disease. Polyunsaturated fats do not raise the level of blood cholesterol and may actually lower it.

In practical terms, the choice is between soft polyunsaturated margarine and butter; many hard margarines contain almost as much saturated fat as butter, while oils of whatever type will not incorporate air when beaten and thus have a limited application in patisserie. Equal quantities of fat, incidentally, contain more or less an equal number of calories.

Dietary considerations alone would dictate the use of polyunsaturated margarine. Taste, however, counsels the use of butter, which has an incomparable flavour. Common sense suggests a compromise. In this volume butter is only specified where its unique qualities make a distinct difference to the final product. All the other recipes recommend the use of polyunsaturated margarine. Obviously, these instructions may be tailored to suit individual needs and preferences.

Certain foods containing cholesterol may contribute to raising blood cholesterol levels. Egg yolks, indispensable to many patisserie creations, contain it in large amounts. Although dietary cholesterol is not so important a contributor to blood cholesterol as that which we make ourselves from saturated fat, it is nonetheless good dietary practice to eat cholesterol-rich foods in moderation. In some preparations, egg yolks traditionally serve as the main binding agent but substitutions can be devised.

The new thinking is demonstrated in the four standard recipes on pages 10 and 11. Patisserie is often assembled from precooked ingredients, and these key recipes provide the bases for the confections that appear later and for your own creations. Genoese, a light sponge, is usually made with a ratio of four eggs to 125 g (4 oz) of flour, but on page 11 one yolk is omitted and an egg white added to help bind the mixture and make it rise. The amount of butter is also less than that usually specified.

Pastry cream, another stand-by of classic French patisserie, is a custard primarily thickened with egg yolks, but the recipe on page 11 replaces some of the egg yolks with cornflour and egg white. The choux dough on page 10 is made with half the eggs usually required and half the butter. The shortcrust dough on the same page is not enriched with eggs and sugar, as in many classic patisserie recipes, and it calls for polyunsaturated margarine. In short, all the cornerstones of classic patisserie have been recreated in a healthier mould.

The right ingredients used correctly.

The lightest sponges, the airiest meringues, the crispest tartlet cases and the most tender choux dough require the most refined ingredients if they are to achieve the sweet and fleeting perfection that is the hallmark of good patisserie. For this reason, sifted white flour is generally used in preference to wholemeal flour, which produces heavier, denser baked goods with a pronounced nutty flavour. White caster sugar is the main sweetening agent for most patisserie; the fine crystals blend easily into doughs and batters. Brown sugars, which are not nutritionally superior to the more refined variety, are sometimes chosen for their more assertive flavour, or to impart a golden colour to a meringue or pastry base. Honey has an advantage over commercial sugars in

that — weight for weight — it possesses one and a half times the sweetening power. It is included in the apple and pear upside-down tartlets on page 17 and the honey and hazelnut tartlets on page 29, but its distinctive flavour rules it out as an all-purpose sweetening agent.

Egg whites play a vital role in imparting lightness to cakes, mousses and fillings without adding fat or cholesterol and at a minimal calorific cost; there are fewer than 20 calories in an egg white. To prepare egg whites for beating, they must be carefully separated from the yolks, which contain fat that prevents the whites from rising properly. Eggs can be separated either by letting the white drip between the fingers into a bowl or by passing the yolk between the halves of the egg shell so that the white falls into the bowl. In either case, if the recipe calls for a number of egg whites, it is wise to drop each white in turn into a small bowl before adding it to the rest; in this way, if a yolk should break and mix with the white, it will not spoil the other whites. Beaters and bowls must be scrupulously clean, and plastic should never be used since it harbours traces of fat. Bowls made of glass, china or — best of all — copper are recommended.

The delicate mousses used as fillings and toppings in this volume are made with low-fat soft cheeses lightened with egg whites and stiffened with gelatine. These have fewer calories than the egg and cream-enriched versions used in traditional patisserie. Powdered gelatine is used in preference to leaf gelatine because it is easier to obtain and to measure.

Fruits are given a prominent place in many of the recipes because of their intrinsic sweetness, vibrant colours and delicious flavours. They are healthy, too — high in fibre, vitamins and minerals and low in calories. Like honey, fruits owe their natural sweetness to the presence of fructose. Choose fresh, ripe fruit. Canned fruits should be avoided since neither their flavour nor their appearance can match those of fresh fruit, but frozen fruits provide adequate substitutes if fresh varieties are out of season. Frozen raspberries, blackberries, cranberries, gooseberries and rhubarb work well in sauces and purées. In many shops and marketplaces, imported tropical fruits are as familiar as home-grown varieties; the general availability of such formerly exotic items as kumquats, passion fruits, Cape gooseberries and kiwi fruits is reflected in the recipes.

Finishing touches

At the tables of the European nobility during the 18th and 19th centuries, patisserie was so heavily and fancifully decorated that one of the greatest *pâtissiers* of the period, Antonin Carême, likened it to architecture rather than cookery. Happily for the home cook, such excessive ornamentation is no longer consid-

The Key to Better Eating

Healthy Home Cooking addresses the concerns of today's weight-conscious, health-minded cooks with recipes that take into account guidelines set by nutritionists. The secret to eating well, of course, has to do with maintaining a balance of foods in the diet. The recipes should therefore be used thoughtfully, in the context of a day's eating. To make the choice easier, this book offers an analysis of the nutrients in each recipe, as on the right. The analysis is for a single cake or pastry, or an individual serving of a larger item. The counts that are given for calories, protein, cholesterol, total fat, saturated fat and sodium are approximate.

Interpreting the chart

The chart below gives dietary guidelines for healthy men, women and children. Recommended figures vary from country to country, but the principles are the same everywhere. Here, the average daily amounts of calories and protein are from a report by the U.K. Department of Health and Social Security; the maximum advisable daily intake of fat is based on guidelines given by the National

---

Calories **220**
Protein **5g**
Cholesterol **60mg**
Total fat **6g**
Saturated fat **3g**
Sodium **20mg**

Advisory Committee on Nutrition Education (NACNE); those for cholesterol and sodium are based on upper limits suggested by the World Health Organization.

The volumes in the Healthy Home Cooking series do not purport to be diet books, nor do they focus on health foods. Rather, they express a commonsense approach to cooking that uses salt, sugar, cream, butter and oil in moderation while employing other ingredients that also provide flavour and satisfaction. In these patisserie recipes, nuts, spices, fruits, peels, juices and spirits are all used towards this end.

In this volume, a conscious effort has been made to limit the cakes, pastries and confectionery to 250 calories per serving, and to restrict the amount of total fat and saturated

fat to 10 and 5 g per helping respectively. Occasionally, in the interest of taste, texture or even the successful cooking of a patisserie, the amount of sugar or fat has been increased. When a recipe exceeds the 250-calorie limit, the cook should cut back a little elsewhere in the daily menu.

The recipes make few unusual demands. Naturally they call for fresh ingredients, offering substitutes when these are unavailable. (Only the original ingredient is calculated in the nutrient analysis, however.) Most of the ingredients can be found in any well-stocked supermarket. Any that may seem unfamiliar are described in a glossary on pages 138 and 139. In order to help the cook master new techniques, how-to photographs and step-by-step instructions appear whenever these are appropriate.

About cooking times

Because the recipes emphasize fresh foods, they may take a bit longer to prepare than dishes that call for packaged products, but the payoff in flavour, and often in nutrition, should compensate for the little extra time involved. To help the cook plan ahead, Healthy Home Cooking provides "working" and "total" times for each recipe.

Working time denotes the minutes actively spent on preparation; however, since no two cooks work at exactly the same speed, it is, of course, approximate. Total time includes any soaking or chilling specified in the recipe, and it includes unattended cooking time; again, because of the variations in oven temperatures and in sizes of cake and tartlet tins, the cooking times given can only be taken as an average. The total time also includes the minutes — or sometimes even the hours — that the finished product takes to cool to room temperature or to set completely. (Cooling and setting times can vary according to the temperature and humidity of the kitchen.)

Recommended Dietary Guidelines

		Average Daily Intake		**Maximum Daily Intake**			
		CALORIES	PROTEIN grams	CHOLESTEROL milligrams	TOTAL FAT grams	SATURATED FAT grams	SODIUM milligrams
Females	7-8	1900	47	300	80	32	2000*
	9-11	2050	51	300	77	35	2000
	12-17	2150	53	300	81	36	2000
	18-53	2150	54	300	81	36	2000
	54-74	1900	47	300	72	32	2000
Males	7-8	1980	49	300	80	33	2000
	9-11	2280	57	300	77	38	2000
	12-14	2640	66	300	99	44	2000
	15-17	2880	72	300	108	48	2000
	18-34	2900	72	300	109	48	2000
	35-64	2750	69	300	104	35	2000
	65-74	2400	60	300	91	40	2000

*(or 5g salt)

ered either necessary or desirable for the creation of beautiful patisserie. The decorations shown on the following pages are both elegant in their simplicity and well within the reach of most cooks, providing a final flourish that does not require hours of labour or add scores of unwanted calories to the product.

A dusting of icing sugar is sufficient embellishment for most small cakes and pastries. Various patterns can be made by masking part of the cake with pieces of card before sprinkling on the sugar. A similar effect but in a different colour may be achieved by using cocoa powder. Icing sugar can be dissolved in water or fruit juice to make a thin glacé icing for spooning or piping over a cake or pastry. Instead of applying a uniform coating, pipe a few threads on the patisserie to create maximum visual effect with minimum calories.

The glossy sheen of a caramel coating can enhance the appearance of both patisserie and confectionery, and the crisp, sweet texture is well worth the effort that making caramel entails. It is prepared by heating sugar with water until the sugar becomes pale brown and fragrant. The cooking process is arrested by dipping the pan in cold water, then the pan is placed in a bowl of hot water to keep the caramel fluid during the time it takes to apply it. It is important to disturb the caramel as little as possible, to prevent it from crystallizing.

Jam, in all its bright colours and sweet flavours, provides an attractive finishing touch. The redcurrant jelly coating on the strawberry tartlets on page 19 intensifies the colour of the fruit and makes it even more jewel-like; apricot jam spread on an apple slice produces a golden glaze that helps bring out the apple's flavour *(page 16)*; raspberry jam piped in a flower pattern makes a delicate embellishment to petits fours *(page 133)*.

Of all the elements used in patisserie, chocolate is the ingredient that for many people most symbolizes luxurious self-indulgence. The richness and smoothness of chocolate is achieved during manufacture by adding extra cocoa butter to the ground beans, which are sweetened by the addition of large quantities of sugar — up to 60 per cent of the final weight — and sometimes given a milder flavour by the addition of milk. Because of the presence of fats, even plain chocolate has a calorific content about one and a half times that of sugar; milk chocolate, with only about 1 per cent more fat, is not significantly higher in calories. The strategy of the health-conscious cook should be to buy the best quality dark chocolate available, which will contain at least 52 per cent cocoa solids and correspondingly less sugar. The stronger flavour of such chocolate means that a little goes a long way.

Even used sparingly, chocolate produces striking decorative effects thanks to its unique consistency. When melted over a gentle heat it liquefies, and in this form can be piped or dribbled into patterns, used as a bath for dipping small cakes and confectionery, or poured into a flat tray where it sets into a thin sheet as it cools. Once set, the chocolate can be cut into squares to make boxes for petits fours *(page 132)* or shaved paper-thin with a sharp knife to make scrolls. These techniques and effects are explained on pages 12 and 13.

Necessary equipment

A kitchen fully equipped for making patisserie may contain a bewildering variety of pans, tins, cutters, piping nozzles and moulds of all shapes and sizes, special tools for stoning cherries and for scraping ribbons of rind from citrus fruits, plus a powerful hand beater and a sturdy food processor. Many of these items, though useful and labour saving, are not absolutely necessary. Food processors and electric beaters certainly save time, but their work can usually be done with the aid of sharp knives, a wooden spoon or a wire whisk, as the case may be. So long as the dimensions of the tin you substitute are the same, tartlets can be made in standard bun tins instead of in the range of exotically shaped tins suggested by the recipes. Cherries can be stoned with a small, sharp knife, and citrus rind can be removed with a vegetable peeler and then cut into shreds.

The truly indispensable implements for making patisserie are accurate kitchen scales and a set of measuring spoons; exact quantities are important to the success of cakes and pastries. While a sugar thermometer is not necessary for some recipes such as caramel, which is easy to judge by eye as the sugar darkens, other stages of sugar syrup, such as soft crack *(page 127)*, are most accurately gauged with a sugar thermometer to ensure that they are neither too sticky nor too brittle.

A good working knowledge of your oven is also essential, for cooking times can vary widely from oven to oven. Cooking times and temperatures given in the recipes are for conventional ovens; if you have a fan-assisted oven, which circulates heat more quickly, keep to the recommended cooking time and reduce the temperature by up to 40°C (75°F). Use your manufacturer's guidelines. Microwave ovens are not only invaluable for preparing some ingredients — such as hard fruits that need cooking – for final assembly, but may also produce finished patisserie in their own right. The recipes on pages 129 to 137 illustrate the versatility of these time-saving machines.

Patisserie may be enjoyed with any meal, but perhaps it is best appreciated on its own, served with tea, coffee or a fruit drink to make a soothing interlude at mid-morning or in the afternoon. By exercising complete control over the ingredients used in home-made patisserie, you can enjoy such welcome moments without departing from a healthy diet.

Four Essential Recipes

Shortcrust Dough

Makes about 275 g (9 oz)
Working (and total) time: about 10 minutes

175 g	plain flour	6 oz
1 tsp	sugar	1 tsp
90 g	polyunsaturated margarine, chilled	3 oz
1	egg white, lightly beaten	1

Sift the flour and sugar into a mixing bowl. Add the margarine and rub it into the dry ingredients with your fingertips until the mixture resembles fine bread-crumbs. Add the egg white and mix it in with a round-bladed knife to form a dough. Gather the dough into a firm ball and knead it briefly on a lightly floured surface until smooth; do not overwork the dough or it will become oily and the baked pastry will be tough. Roll out the dough as required.

EDITOR'S NOTE: *Shortcrust dough may be stored, wrapped in plastic film, in the refrigerator for up to a week or in the freezer for up to three months.*

Choux Dough

Working (and total) time: about 15 minutes

125 g	plain flour	4 oz
⅛ tsp	salt	⅛ tsp
75 g	unsalted butter	2½ oz
2	eggs	2
1	egg white	1

Sift the flour and salt on to a sheet of greaseproof paper. Put the butter and ¼ litre (8 fl oz) of water into a heavy-bottomed pan and heat gently until the butter melts. Increase the heat to medium high and bring to the boil. Remove the pan from the heat and slide in all the flour, beating vigorously with a wooden spoon. Return to the heat and continue beating the mixture until it forms a ball. Allow to cool for a few minutes.

Lightly beat the eggs and egg white together. Using an electric hand-held mixer, or beating vigorously with a wooden spoon, gradually incorporate the eggs into the cooled mixture. Beat well after each addition and continue until the mixture forms a smooth shiny paste.

EDITOR'S NOTE: *Uncooked choux dough does not keep; it should be prepared and used as required. Once cooked, however, choux buns may be frozen, then thawed and filled at a later date. The recipes in Chapter 1 calling for choux dough either use the full quantity made here or, if less is required, list the necessary ingredients within the individual recipe ingredients lists.*

Genoese Sponge

Makes one 30 by 20 cm (12 by 8 inch) sponge
Working time: about 20 minutes
Total time: about 1 hour

3	eggs	3
1	egg white	1
90 g	caster sugar	3 oz
125 g	plain flour	4 oz
30 g	unsalted butter, melted and cooled slightly	1 oz

Preheat the oven to 180°C (350°F or Mark 4). Butter a 30 by 20 by 4 cm (12 by 8 by 1½ inch) rectangular tin and line the base with non-stick parchment paper.

Put the eggs, egg white and caster sugar into a mixing bowl. Set the bowl over a saucepan of hot, but not boiling, water on a low heat. Using an electric hand-held mixer, whisk the eggs and sugar together until thick and very pale. Remove the bowl from the saucepan and continue whisking until the mixture is cool and falls from the whisk in a ribbon trail. Sift the flour very lightly over the surface of the egg and sugar mixture, then fold it in gently using a large metal spoon. Gradually fold in the melted butter.

Pour the sponge batter into the prepared tin and spread it evenly. Bake it for 25 to 30 minutes, until well risen, springy to the touch and very slightly shrunk from the sides of the tin. Carefully unmould the sponge on to a wire rack. Loosen the parchment paper but do not remove it. Place another wire rack on top of the paper, then invert both racks together so that the sponge is right side up on top of the paper. Remove the top rack and allow the sponge to cool.

EDITOR'S NOTE: *Individual recipes do not always use the full quantity of sponge prepared here. Leftover sponge may be stored in an airtight tin for several days and used on another occasion; several of the recipes in Chapter 3 make use of sponge trimmings.*

Pastry Cream

Makes about 30 cl (½ pint)
Working time: about 25 minutes
Total time: about 1 hour and 50 minutes (includes chilling)

2	egg yolks	2
30 g	caster sugar	1 oz
30 g	plain flour, sifted	1 oz
15 g	cornflour, sifted	½ oz
30 cl	skimmed milk	½ pint
1 tsp	pure vanilla extract	1 tsp
2 tbsp	thick Greek yogurt	2 tbsp
1	egg white	1

Put the egg yolks and half the caster sugar into a bowl. Whisk them together until thick, then carefully fold in the flour and cornflour.

Heat the milk and vanilla extract together in a saucepan until hot but not boiling. Gradually whisk the hot milk into the egg mixture, then strain the mixture through a nylon sieve back into the pan. Stir the custard over a low heat until it comes to the boil, then simmer it, stirring continuously, for 5 to 6 minutes, or until no taste of raw flour remains, do not let the custard burn during this time. Remove the pan from the heat, spoon the custard into a bowl and cover the surface closely with plastic film to prevent a skin forming. Allow to cool for about 10 minutes, then refrigerate until almost, but not quite, cold — 15 to 20 minutes.

Whisk the custard until it is smooth, then whisk in the yogurt. In another bowl, whisk the egg white until stiff, then whisk in the remaining sugar until shiny. Gradually fold the egg white into the custard. Cover the bowl with plastic film and chill the pastry cream for at least 1 hour.

Orange-flavoured pastry cream. Add the finely grated rind of one orange to the milk. Whisk 1 tablespoon of Grand Marnier into the cooled custard before adding the whisked egg white.

Chocolate-flavoured pastry cream. Melt 30 g (1 oz) of plain chocolate in the hot milk in the saucepan.

Liqueur-flavoured pastry cream. Whisk 1 tablespoon of rum, brandy or liqueur such as Cointreau, kirsch or Tia Maria into the cooled custard before adding the whisked egg white.

EDITOR'S NOTE: *The pastry cream may be stored in the refrigerator for up to two days.*

Making Chocolate Go Further

For the health-conscious *pâtissier* chocolate poses a challenge. Greatly desirable for its incomparable flavour and luxurious smoothness, it is undeniably high in fat and calories: 30 g (1 oz) of plain chocolate contain 143 calories and 10 g of fat, of which 6 g are saturated fat. The creative answer to this dilemma is to make chocolate go a long way.

In place of a thick chocolate icing, a sprinkling of grated chocolate provides an appetizing finish for patisserie. For decoration, you can also shave chocolate into scrolls *(right)*, cut a thin sheet into geometric shapes *(below)*, or pipe it into edible embroidery *(opposite page)* using a greaseproof paper piping bag.

Chocolate easily scorches if exposed to direct heat. To melt chocolate, break it into pieces and place the pieces in a heatproof bowl. Fill a pan a quarter full of water and bring it to a simmer. Set the bowl over the pan. Stir the chocolate with a wooden spoon until it is smooth.

Miniature Scrolls

1 SPREADING CHOCOLATE. Brush a work surface with oil to prevent sticking. Melt chocolate in a bowl set over hot water, then pour the chocolate on to the work surface. Using a flexible metal spatula, spread the chocolate as thinly as possible *(above)*; leave it to cool and set.

2 FORMING THE SCROLLS. Push the edge of a knife blade or a stiff, wide-bladed scraper into the chocolate at a low angle. Use a continuous motion to roll the chocolate into a scroll.

Smooth Squares and Rectangles

1 SMOOTHING THE CHOCOLATE. Grease a Swiss roll tin and line it with greaseproof paper. Melt chocolate in a bowl set over hot water and pour it into the tin to form a layer 2 mm (1/10 inch) deep. Rap the tin on the work surface to eliminate air bubbles, then smooth the chocolate with a flexible metal spatula *(above)*.

2 UNMOULDING THE SHEET. Leave the chocolate to harden in a cool place for about 30 minutes. Place a sheet of greaseproof paper on the surface; invert the tin. Lift the tin and peel away the lining paper *(above)*.

3 CUTTING THE SHAPES. Using a long, sharp knife or cutters, cut the chocolate into the desired shapes — here 4 cm (1½ inch) squares. For squares or rectangles, use a ruler to measure the intervals and nick the edges of the chocolate sheet with the tip of a small, sharp knife.

Delicate Tracery

1 *CUTTING A TRIANGLE. Cut out a 30 cm 12 inch) square of greaseproof paper. Fold the square in half diagonally, then cut along the crease (above). Reserve one triangle.*

2 *FOLDING THE TRIANGLE. Place a triangle on the work surface with its right angle at the bottom right-hand corner. Place the fingers of your left hand on the middle of the edge nearest you and grasp the left-hand corner with your right hand; pull it over your left hand to meet the right-angled corner (above).*

3 *MAKING A CONE. Tuck the two corners under the fingers of your left hand. With your right hand grasp the corner furthest from you and wrap it around your left hand to make a cone with a fine point (above). Fold the three corners down together. Fill the paper cone two-thirds full with melted chocolate.*

4 *SEALING THE PIPING BAG. Fold the top edge of the piping bag down to close the opening (above, left). Fold the corners towards the middle, then fold the top edge of the bag down again (above, right). Snip off the tip of the bag to make the size of hole required: the smaller the hole, the finer the line of decoration will be.*

5 *PIPING THE CHOCOLATE. Hold the piping bag between your fingers and thumb, at an angle of 45 degrees to the surface and just above it. Squeeze gently and pipe towards yourself, raising the bag slightly as the chocolate falls on to the surface (above). For a zigzag effect, move the bag from side to side. To finish, lower the tip and pull away sharply.*

1 *Crisp pastry cases stand ready to be filled with a selection of colourful fresh fruits (recipe, page 20).*

Happy Unions of Pastry and Filling

Patisserie is, literally, the creation of the pastry cook, and at the heart of classic patisserie are the pastries themselves — the perfect foil for velvety creams and custards, chocolate and caramel, fruit and nuts. Because puff and flaky pastries depend for their success on a high butter content they have no place in a volume on healthy cooking. But shortcrust, choux and phyllo pastries make such adaptable foundations that the omissions will cause no hardship.

Shortcrust, the basis of crisp tartlet shells, is simplicity itself to make, requiring only cool ingredients mixed with a light hand for perfect results. Polyunsaturated margarine, which remains soft even at fairly low temperatures, must be thoroughly chilled. Rub it gently into the flour with the fingertips only, lifting and sifting the flour at the same time. As soon as the mixture looks like breadcrumbs, stop rubbing or it will become oily. Egg white rather than water is used to bind the dry ingredients, which reduces shrinkage when the dough is baked. The dough should be rolled no more than is necessary; shortcrust pastry that is overworked becomes tough.

Patient preparation is the only requisite for choux pastry, the starting point for the tender éclairs, puffs and fingers on pages 34 to 47. Add the eggs a little at a time, beating vigorously between each addition to incorporate as much air as possible. Your reward comes when the choux dough is baked, rising to four times its original volume, or even more if it is cooked in an enclosed steamy atmosphere as in the recipe for peach choux puffs on page 36.

Once baked, choux pastry cases can be kept in a cool place, covered with foil, for up to 8 hours before filling. They will soften quickly when filled, so prepare them for the table no more than 1 to 2 hours before serving, or as the recipe directs.

Phyllo, a traditional Middle Eastern pastry, has a low fat content and a subtle flavour, making it the perfect partner for richly spiced fruit-and-nut mixtures. Used paper-thin and built up in layers, it can be formed into any number of shapes — from simple rolled strudel (page 52) to fans (page 48), cigars (page 58) and petal cases filled with fruit (page 59).

Apple Slice

THIS IS A VARIATION ON THE TRADITIONAL FRENCH APPLE
TART: HERE, THE DELICATE FLAVOUR OF LIME ADDS SUBTLETY
TO THE APPLE FILLING.

Serves 8
Working time: about 45 minutes
Total time: about 2 hours and 20 minutes

Calories **260**
Protein **3g**
Cholesterol **0mg**
Total fat **11g**
Saturated fat **2g**
Sodium **100mg**

150 g	wholemeal flour	5 oz
1 tsp	light brown sugar	1 tsp
90 g	polyunsaturated margarine, chilled	3 oz
30 g	shelled hazelnuts, toasted, skinned (page 29) and ground	1 oz
1	egg white	1
1 tbsp	apricot jam, without added sugar	1 tbsp
Apple-lime filling		
1 kg	cooking apples, peeled, cored and sliced	2 lb
1	lime, grated rind and juice	1
90 g	caster sugar	3 oz
2	dessert apples	2
2 tsp	icing sugar	2 tsp

Lightly butter a 35 by 11 cm (14 by 4½ inch) loose-based fluted or plain tart tin.

To make the dough, sift the flour and sugar into a mixing bowl. Rub in the margarine with your fingertips until the mixture resembles fine breadcrumbs. With a round-bladed knife, blend in the ground hazelnuts and the egg white. Knead the dough briefly on a lightly floured surface until it is smooth, then roll it out into a rectangle 2.5 cm (1 inch) larger all round than the tart tin. Lift the dough with the rolling pin and ease it into the tin, pressing it into the fluted edges. Trim off excess dough with a knife and prick the inside with a fork. Chill while preparing the filling.

Preheat the oven to 190°C (375°F or Mark 5). To make the filling, place the cooking apples in a large, non-reactive saucepan with the grated lime rind, half the lime juice and 2 tablespoons of water. Cover, bring to the boil, then cook gently, stirring occasionally, until the apples are tender and pulpy. Stir in the caster sugar and boil off any excess juice, then set the pan aside to cool. Peel, core and thinly slice the dessert apples. Toss the slices in the remaining lime juice to prevent discoloration.

Spread the cooked apple mixture in the dough case and arrange overlapping apple slices on top. Sift the icing sugar over the apple slices. Place the tin on a baking sheet and bake the tart in the oven until the pastry is golden-brown and the apple slices have browned at the edges — 30 to 40 minutes.

In a small pan set over gentle heat, warm the apricot jam with a tablespoon of water until liquid. Press the liquid jam through a nylon sieve, then use a pastry brush to paint the glaze over the apple slices.

Allow the tart to cool fully in the tin, then carefully unmould it and cut it in slices for serving.

Apple and Pear Upside-Down Tartlets

BECAUSE THE TARTLETS ARE BAKED UPSIDE DOWN, THE PASTRY REMAINS CRISP AS THE FRUIT BELOW IS COOKED BY THE HEAT OF THE OVEN CONDUCTED THROUGH THE TIN.

Makes 6 tartlets
Working time: about 35 minutes
Total time: about 1 hour and 10 minutes

Per tartlet:
Calories **210**
Protein **3g**
Cholesterol **0mg**
Total fat **8g**
Saturated fat **2g**
Sodium **100mg**

175 g	shortcrust dough (recipe, page 10), made with ¾ teaspoon ground cinnamon added to dry ingredients	6 oz
2 tbsp	clear honey	2 tbsp
3	small dessert apples	3
3	small dessert pears	3
2 tsp	fresh lemon juice	2 tsp

Wrap the shortcrust dough in plastic film and chill it while making the filling.

Preheat the oven to 200°C (400°F or Mark 6). Lightly butter six 10 cm (4 inch) fluted tartlet tins. Boil the honey in a small saucepan for 1 minute. Pour a little hot honey into the buttered tins, evenly coating their bottoms. Peel, core and thinly slice the fruit, and toss the slices in the lemon juice to prevent discoloration. Arrange alternate layers of apples and pears in each tin, overlapping the slices in each layer. (Arrange the bottom layer of slices particularly carefully; this will be the top when the tartlets are inverted.) The layered fruit should rise slightly above the top of the tin.

Cut the dough into six equal pieces and roll out each piece on a lightly floured surface into a circle a little wider than the top of a tartlet tin. Neaten the edges, then place the dough circles over the fruit, tucking their edges inside the tins. Seal the dough to the fluted rims of the tins by pressing with your fingers all round the inside edges.

Bake the tartlets until the pastry is golden-brown — 25 to 30 minutes. Leave them in their tins for a few minutes, then invert them on to serving plates. Serve the tartlets warm or cold.

EDITOR'S NOTE: *If liked, a little extra honey can be dribbled over the top of the tartlets for serving.*

Jam Tartlets

Makes 18 tartlets
Working time: about 25 minutes
Total time: about 1 hour and 10 minutes

Per tartlet:
Calories **95**
Protein **1g**
Cholesterol **0mg**
Total fat **4g**
Saturated fat **1g**
Sodium **45mg**

275 g	shortcrust dough (recipe, page 10)	9 oz
125 g	red jam (strawberry, raspberry, or blackcurrant) without added sugar	4 oz
125 g	apricot jam without added sugar	4 oz
1	glacé pear, thinly sliced	1
1	glacé fig, thinly sliced	1

On a lightly floured surface, roll out the dough to a thickness of 3 mm (⅛ inch). Cut out 18 circles with a 7.5 cm (3 inch) pastry cutter, reserving the dough trimmings. Ease the circles into 6 cm (2½ inch) tartlet tins, prick the insides with a fork, then chill them for 30 minutes. Meanwhile, preheat the oven to 220°C (425°F or Mark 7).

Roll out the reserved pastry trimmings and cut them into petal or diamond shapes with a sharp knife. Put the shapes on a baking sheet and bake them together with the chilled tartlet cases. Remove the cases from the oven after 7 minutes; leave the shapes for a further 2 to 3 minutes, until they are golden-brown.

Spoon 2 rounded teaspoons of red jam into half the tartlet cases and decorate with the pear slices. Fill the remaining cases with the apricot jam and top with the fig slices. Return the tartlets to the oven and bake them until the pastry is golden-brown and the jam is bubbling — 5 to 7 minutes.

Unmould the tartlets on to a wire rack to cool. Before serving, decorate them with the pastry shapes.

Strawberry Tartlets

Makes 18 tartlets
Working time: about 25 minutes
Total time: about 1 hour and 10 minutes

Per tartlet:
Calories **95**
Protein **1g**
Cholesterol **0mg**
Total fat **4g**
Saturated fat **1g**
Sodium **45mg**

275 g	shortcrust dough (recipe, page 10)	9 oz
300 g	strawberries, hulled and halved	10 oz
6 tbsp	redcurrant jelly	6 tbsp
1½ tbsp	Pernod or other anise-flavoured spirit	1½ tbsp

On a lightly floured surface, roll out the dough to a thickness of 3 mm (⅛ inch). Using a 7.5 cm (3 inch) cutter, cut 18 circles and use these to line 6 cm (2½ inch) tartlet tins. Prick the insides with a fork, then chill the cases for 30 minutes. Meanwhile, preheat the oven to 220°C (425°F or Mark 7).

Bake the tartlet cases for 15 to 20 minutes, until they are golden-brown. Remove them from the oven, allow them to cool a little, then unmould them on to a wire rack set over a tray.

Arrange the halved strawberries in the tartlet cases. To prepare the glaze, place the redcurrant jelly in a small, non-reactive pan with 1½ tablespoons of water. Stir over gentle heat until the jelly has melted, then stir in the Pernod. Using a pastry brush, paint a generous amount of warm glaze over the strawberries in each tartlet; reheat it if it begins to set.

Fresh Fruit Tartlets with Passion Fruit Cream

Makes 12 tartlets
Working time: about 45 minutes
Total time: about 1 hour and 15 minutes

Per tartlet:
Calories **140**
Protein **3g**
Cholesterol **trace**
Total fat **7g**
Saturated fat **2g**
Sodium **75mg**

275 g	shortcrust dough (recipe, page 10)	9 oz
½	mango	½
½	kiwi fruit	½
12	small strawberries	12
2	kumquats	2
12	green grapes	12
½	pomegranate	½
1	passion fruit	1
Passion fruit cream		
1	passion fruit	1
125 g	fromage frais	4 oz
1 tsp	caster sugar	1 tsp

On a lightly floured surface, roll out the dough to a thickness of about 3 mm (⅛ inch). Cut out 12 circles with a 10 cm (4 inch) pastry cutter and ease them into 7.5 cm (3 inch) shallow tartlet tins. Prick the insides with a fork and chill the cases for 30 minutes. Meanwhile, preheat the oven to 220°C (425°F or Mark 7).

Bake the chilled tartlet cases until they are light brown — 15 to 20 minutes. Allow them to cool a little before unmoulding them on to a wire rack.

While the tartlet cases are baking, prepare the fruit. Peel and thinly slice the mango and kiwi fruit; hull and halve the strawberries; thinly slice the kumquats and remove the seeds; halve and pip the grapes; remove the pomegranate seeds; cut the passion fruit in half widthwise and spoon out the pulp and seeds.

To prepare the passion fruit cream, cut the fruit in half, spoon out the pulp and seeds and blend into the *fromage frais*. Add the sugar and beat until smoothly blended. Spoon the fruit cream into the pastry shells.

Decorate the tartlets with the prepared fresh fruit, filling any gaps with the passion fruit.

EDITOR'S NOTE: *If you are not serving the tartlets immediately, brush the fruit with an apricot glaze: in a small, non-reactive pan, heat 2 tablespoons of apricot jam without added sugar with 2 tablespoons of water, then press the liquid jam through a nylon sieve. Eat the tartlets within a day of preparation.*

Muscat Grape Tartlets

Makes 12 tartlets
Working time: about 35 minutes
Total time: about 2 hours (includes chilling)

Per tartlet:
Calories **140**
Protein **3g**
Cholesterol **trace**
Total fat **6g**
Saturated fat **2g**
Sodium **70mg**

275 g	shortcrust dough (recipe, page 10)	9 oz
24	Muscat grapes or other large firm green grapes	24
4 tbsp	thick Greek yogurt	4 tbsp
Wine syrup		
15 cl	sweet white dessert wine	¼ pint
1 tbsp	sugar	1 tbsp
½	orange, rind only, cut into several pieces	½
1½ tsp	powdered gelatine	1½ tsp

Roll out the dough on a lightly floured surface to a thickness of 3 mm (⅛ inch). Using a sharp knife, cut the dough into twelve 11 by 9 cm (4½ by 3½ inch) rectangles and use these to line 12 oval tartlet tins measuring approximately 7.5 by 5 by 2 cm (3 by 2 by ¾ inch). Prick the insides with a fork and chill the tartlet cases for 30 minutes. Preheat the oven to 220°C (425°F or Mark 7).

Bake the tartlet cases for 15 to 20 minutes, until the pastry is lightly browned. Remove from the oven, cool slightly and unmould on to a wire rack.

Meanwhile, prepare the wine syrup. Put the wine, sugar and orange rind into a small, non-reactive saucepan and heat gently, stirring with a wooden spoon, until the sugar has dissolved. Bring the mixture almost to the boil, then remove it from the heat and allow it to stand, covered, for 30 minutes, so the syrup becomes infused with the flavour of the orange rind.

Using a slotted spoon, remove the orange rind from the syrup. Sprinkle the gelatine over 2 tablespoons of water in a small bowl and leave it to soften for 2 minutes. Set the bowl over a pan of simmering water and stir until the gelatine has fully dissolved. Whisk the warm gelatine into the wine mixture, then chill the syrup until it is beginning to set — about 30 minutes.

Cut the grapes in half and remove the pips. Place 1 teaspoon of yogurt into each pastry case, arrange four grape halves on top, then pour on a little of the wine syrup, shaking the tartlets gently to encourage the syrup to fill the spaces between grapes. Brush any remaining syrup over the surface of the grapes. Chill the tartlets for 20 to 30 minutes, until set, then serve them as soon as possible.

Fig Flowers

Makes 16 flowers
Working time: about 40 minutes
Total time: about 1 hour and 20 minutes

Per flower:
Calories **105**
Protein **2g**
Cholesterol **0mg**
Total fat **7g**
Saturated fat **1g**
Sodium **80mg**

150 g	plain flour	5 oz
30 g	cornmeal	1 oz
1 tsp	caster sugar	1 tsp
90 g	polyunsaturated margarine, chilled	3 oz
1	egg white	1
	Creamy fig filling	
5	ripe figs, quartered lengthwise	5
125 g	medium-fat soft cheese	4 oz
1 tbsp	plain low-fat yogurt	1 tbsp
1 tsp	rose-water	1 tsp
1 tsp	sugar	1 tsp

To make the dough, sift the flour, cornmeal and sugar into a mixing bowl, then rub in the margarine with your fingertips until the mixture resembles fine bread-crumbs. Mix in the egg white with a round-bladed knife, then gather the dough into a ball and knead it briefly on a lightly floured surface until smooth.

Roll the dough out to a thickness of about 3 mm (⅛ inch) and cut out 16 shapes with a 7.5 cm (3 inch) flower cutter. Fit the shapes into 7.5 cm (3 inch) tartlet tins, easing the dough across the base and up the sides of the tins without spoiling the petals. Prick the insides with a fork and chill the flower-shaped cases for 30 minutes. Meanwhile, preheat the oven to 190°C (375°F or Mark 5).

Bake the tartlet cases until they are lightly browned at the edges — 7 to 10 minutes. Allow them to cool slightly, then turn them out on to a wire rack and leave them to cool fully.

To fill the tartlets, cut the fig quarters lengthwise into thin slices, and arrange the slices in the pastry flowers to look like petals. Using a wooden spoon, mix together the soft cheese, yogurt, rose-water and sugar until the mixture becomes smooth and creamy. Transfer the cheese mixture to a piping bag fitted with a 5 mm (¼ inch) star nozzle and pipe a mound of filling into the centre of each fig flower.

Orange Tartlets

Makes 24 tartlets
Working time: about 1 hour
Total time: about 2 hours

Per tartlet:
Calories **90**
Protein **2g**
Cholesterol **20mg**
Total fat **5g**
Saturated fat **1g**
Sodium **45mg**

275 g	shortcrust dough (recipe, page 10)	9 oz
30 cl	orange-flavoured pastry cream (recipe, page 11)	½ pint
4	oranges, rind and pith cut off, segmented (page 41), segments halved lengthwise, 1 tablespoon juice reserved	4
1 tbsp	shred-free orange marmalade	1 tbsp
30 g	shelled pistachio nuts, skinned and thinly sliced	1 oz

Roll out the dough on a lightly floured surface to a thickness of 3 mm (⅛ inch). Using a 7 cm (2¾ inch) fluted cutter, cut out rounds from the dough and use these to line twenty-four 6 cm (2½ inch) tartlet tins or bun tin trays. (The rounds of dough do not completely fill the tins because the tartlets should be shallow.) Using a fork, lightly prick the insides of the tartlet cases and refrigerate them for 30 minutes. Meanwhile, preheat the oven to 220°C (425°F or Mark 7).

Bake the tartlet cases until lightly browned — 15 to 20 minutes. Allow them to cool a little in the tins, then unmould them on to wire racks to cool fully.

Spoon or pipe the pastry cream into the tartlet cases, then arrange the orange slices neatly on top. Put the reserved orange juice in a small, non-reactive saucepan with the orange marmalade. Gently heat until the mixture comes to the boil. Cook for 1 minute, then use a pastry brush to paint the glaze evenly over the oranges. Sprinkle with the pistachio nuts.

The tartlets may be served in trimmed-down paper baking cases. Eat them the day they are prepared.

EDITOR'S NOTE: *To skin pistachio nuts, blanch them in boiling water for 1 minute, drain them thoroughly, then rub them vigorously in a towel.*

Cherry Custard Tartlets

Makes 12 tartlets
Working time: about 20 minutes
Total time: about 1 hour and 10 minutes

Per tartlet:
Calories **95**
Protein **2g**
Cholesterol **15mg**
Total fat **5g**
Saturated fat **2g**
Sodium **50mg**

275 g	shortcrust dough (recipe, page 10)	9 oz
1	egg	1
1 tbsp	caster sugar	1 tbsp
⅛ tsp	ground cinnamon	⅛ tsp
5 tbsp	single cream	5 tbsp
2 tbsp	skimmed milk	2 tbsp
24	sweet cherries (about 175 g/6 oz), stoned	24

On a lightly floured surface, roll out the dough to a thickness of 5 mm (¼ inch). Cut out 12 circles with a 10 cm (4 inch) cutter, and use them to line deep 6 cm (2½ inch) tartlet tins. Prick the insides with a fork, then chill the tartlet cases for 30 minutes. Meanwhile, preheat the oven to 220°C (425°F or Mark 7).

Arrange the tartlet cases on a baking sheet and bake for 5 minutes. Whisk together the egg, sugar, cinnamon, cream and milk.

Put two cherries into each tartlet case, then pour in the custard mixture. Return the tartlets to the oven and bake until the custard is set and just beginning to brown — about 20 minutes. Serve warm or cold.

Lemon Meringue Barquettes

Makes 20 barquettes
Working time: about 1 hour
Total time: about 2 hours and 30 minutes

Per barquette:
Calories **110**
Protein **2g**
Cholesterol **15mg**
Total fat **4g**
Saturated fat **1g**
Sodium **45mg**

275 g	*shortcrust dough (recipe, page 10)*	9 oz
	Lemon filling	
2	*lemons, rind thinly pared,* *juice strained*	2
45 g	*cornflour*	1½ oz
30 g	*caster sugar*	1 oz
1	*egg yolk*	1
	Meringue topping	
60 g	*caster sugar*	2 oz
60 g	*icing sugar*	2 oz
2	*egg whites*	2

First, begin preparing the filling. Put the lemon rind into a non-reactive saucepan with 30 cl (½ pint) of water. Bring the liquid to the boil, then remove the saucepan from the heat. Cover and allow the mixture to stand for at least 30 minutes, to infuse the lemon rind.

On a lightly floured surface, roll out the dough to a thickness of 3 mm (⅛ inch). Cut the dough into twenty 12 by 7 cm (5 by 2 ¾ inch) rectangles, and use these to line 10 by 4.5 cm (4 by 1 ¾ inch) barquette tins. Lightly prick the inside of each case with a fork, then chill them for 30 minutes. Meanwhile, preheat the oven to 220°C (425°F or Mark 7).

Bake the barquette cases until the pastry is very lightly browned — 20 to 25 minutes. Allow the cases to cool a little in their tins, then carefully unmould them on to a large baking sheet. Set them aside while completing the filling. Leave the oven on.

Using a slotted spoon, remove the lemon rind from the saucepan, then stir in the lemon juice. In a small bowl, blend the cornflour with a little of the lemon liquid to form a smooth cream, then stir it into the saucepan. Bring the mixture to the boil, stirring continuously until it thickens and clears. Continue cooking over a low heat until no taste of raw cornflour remains — 2 to 3 minutes. Remove the saucepan from the heat, then beat the caster sugar and egg yolk into the lemon mixture. Spoon the lemon filling into the barquette cases, filling them to just below their tops.

To make the meringue topping, sift the caster sugar and icing sugar together into a bowl. In a separate bowl, whisk the egg whites until they are stiff but not dry. Gradually whisk the sugar into the egg whites, 1 level tablespoon at a time, whisking well between each addition to make a stiff, shiny meringue.

Spoon the meringue into a piping bag fitted with an 8 mm (⅓ inch) star nozzle and pipe the meringue decoratively on top of the lemon filling in each pastry case. Alternatively, spoon on the meringue, smoothing it with the back of a teaspoon. Bake the barquettes until the meringue just begins to turn light brown — 4 to 5 minutes. Allow the barquettes to cool, then refrigerate them for 30 minutes before serving.

Lemon Curd Tartlets

Makes 18 tartlets
Working time: about 35 minutes
Total time: about 1 hour and 15 minutes

Per tartlet:
Calories **125**
Protein **3g**
Cholesterol **15mg**
Total fat **10g**
Saturated fat **2g**
Sodium **110mg**

275 g	shortcrust dough (recipe, page 10)	9 oz
175 g	curd cheese	6 oz
1	lemon, grated rind only	1
1½ tbsp	fresh lemon juice	1½ tbsp
1½ tbsp	clear honey	1½ tbsp
1	egg, lightly beaten	1
1	egg white	1
15 g	fresh breadcrumbs	½ oz
15 g	flaked almonds	½ oz
Sugar icing		
½	lightly whisked egg white	½
60 g	icing sugar, sifted	2 oz

On a lightly floured surface, roll out the shortcrust dough to a thickness of about 3 mm (⅛ inch). Using a 7.5 cm (3 inch) cutter, cut out 18 circles and use these circles to line 6 cm (2½ inch) tartlet tins or bun tin trays. Prick the insides of the tartlet cases with a fork, then chill the cases for about 15 minutes. Preheat the oven to 200°C (400°F or Mark 6).

Meanwhile, make the lemon curd filling. Beat the curd cheese with the lemon rind and juice, and the honey, then mix in the whole egg, egg white and breadcrumbs. Spoon this mixture into the chilled pastry cases, filling them two-thirds full. Sprinkle a few almond flakes over the top of each.

To make the icing, mix the lightly whisked egg white and icing sugar together until smooth, then spoon a little over each tartlet. Bake the tartlets for about 20 minutes, until risen and golden. Unmould the tartlets on to a wire rack, and allow them to cool for 10 to 15 minutes before serving.

Redcurrant Meringue Squares

Makes 24 squares
Working time: about 40 minutes
Total time: about 4 hours and 30 minutes

Per square:
Calories **90**
Protein **1g**
Cholesterol **0mg**
Total fat **3g**
Saturated fat **1g**
Sodium **40mg**

275 g	shortcrust dough (recipe, page 10)	9 oz
750 g	redcurrants, picked over	1½ lb
175 g	caster sugar	6 oz
1 tbsp	cornflour	1 tbsp
2	egg whites	2

Roll the dough out into a rectangle on a lightly floured surface and trim it to line the base of a 30 by 20 cm (12 by 8 inch) baking tin. Lift the dough on a rolling pin and ease it into the tin, pressing it down gently. Prick the dough with a fork and chill it for 30 minutes. Meanwhile, preheat the oven to 220°C (425°F or Mark 7).

Bake the pastry for 20 to 25 minutes, until lightly browned, then remove it from the oven and reduce the oven temperature to 70°C (160°F or Mark ¼).

Put the redcurrants with 90 g (3 oz) of the sugar in a non-reactive saucepan. Cook over a low heat until the berries are soft and the mixture is liquid — 4 to 5 minutes. Blend the cornflour with 1 tablespoon of water, stirring to form a smooth paste. Add the cornflour paste to the redcurrants, bring to the boil and cook, stirring, until the mixture thickens and clears — about 2 minutes. Spread the redcurrant mixture over the cooked pastry base.

Whisk the egg whites until they form peaks, then gradually whisk in the remaining sugar until the mixture is stiff and glossy. Transfer the meringue to a piping bag fitted with an 8 mm (⅓ inch) star nozzle, and pipe a diagonal lattice pattern over the redcurrants. Bake the tart for 2 hours, then turn off the heat and allow the tart to cool inside the oven. Cut the tart into twenty-four 5 cm (2 inch) squares for serving.

Cranberry Meringue Tartlets

Makes 18 tartlets
Working time: about 1 hour
Total time: about 2 hours

Per tartlet:
Calories **115**
Protein **2g**
Cholesterol **0mg**
Total fat **4g**
Saturated fat **1g**
Sodium **50mg**

275 g	shortcrust dough (recipe, page 10)	9 oz
Fruit filling		
175 g	fresh cranberries, picked over, or frozen cranberries, thawed	6 oz
3 tbsp	fresh orange juice	3 tbsp
2 tbsp	clear honey	2 tbsp
30 g	caster sugar	1 oz
½ tsp	arrowroot	½ tsp
Meringue topping		
2	egg whites	2
125 g	caster sugar	4 oz

On a lightly floured surface, roll out the dough to a thickness of 3 mm (⅛ inch). Using a 7.5 cm (3 inch) cutter, stamp out 18 rounds and use these to line 6 cm (2½ inch) tartlet tins. Prick the insides with a fork, then chill the tartlet cases for 30 minutes. Meanwhile, preheat the oven to 220°C (425°F or Mark 7).

Stand the tins on a baking sheet and bake the pastry cases for 15 to 20 minutes, until they are lightly browned and crisp. Remove from the oven, allow the cases to cool in the tins slightly, then unmould them on to a baking sheet. Reduce the oven temperature to 150°C (300°F or Mark 2).

While the pastry cases are baking, make the fruit filling. Put the cranberries into a small, non-reactive saucepan with the orange juice and cook gently, covered, for about 8 minutes, until the fruit is soft and all the berries have "popped". Stir in the honey and sugar, then add the arrowroot blended with 2 teaspoons of cold water. Bring the mixture back to the boil, stirring until it has thickened, then remove the pan from the heat and allow the filling to cool. Spoon the cooled cranberry mixture into the pastry cases.

To make the topping, whisk the egg whites until they form peaks, then whisk in the sugar, a tablespoon at a time, until the meringue is stiff and glossy. Transfer the meringue to a piping bag fitted with a 1 cm (½ inch) star nozzle and pipe a whirl on top of each tart to completely cover the filling. Return the tartlets to the oven and bake them for about 10 minutes, until the meringue is lightly tinged a pale brown.

Cherry Bakewell Barquettes

THIS RECIPE IS IDEAL FOR USING UP SPONGE CAKE TRIMMINGS.

Makes: 30 barquettes
Working time: about 1 hour
Total time: about 1 hour and 40 minutes

Per barquette:
Calories **95**
Protein **1g**
Cholesterol **10mg**
Total fat **5g**
Saturated fat **1g**
Sodium **50mg**

275 g	shortcrust dough (recipe, page 10)	9 oz
4 tbsp	red jam (raspberry, strawberry or black cherry) without added sugar	4 tbsp
3 tbsp	apricot jam without added sugar	3 tbsp
4	glacé cherries, finely chopped	4
½ oz	pine-nuts, lightly toasted	½ oz
Almond filling		
60 g	polyunsaturated margarine	2 oz
30 g	caster sugar	1 oz
½ tsp	pure almond extract	½ tsp
1	egg, beaten	1
60 g	sponge cake crumbs	2 oz
30 g	ground almonds	1 oz

Roll out the dough on a lightly floured surface to a thickness of 3 mm (⅛ inch). Cut out thirty 10 by 5 cm (4 by 2 inch) rectangles and use these to line 8.5 by 4 cm (3½ by 1½ inch) barquette tins. Press the dough firmly into the tins and trim the edges. Place the tins on a baking sheet and chill them for 30 minutes.

Meanwhile, preheat the oven to 220°C (425°F or Mark 7) and prepare the filling. Put the margarine and sugar together in a small mixing bowl and beat them well until creamy. Beat in the almond extract, then gradually beat in the egg. Add the sponge cake crumbs and ground almonds and fold them in lightly with a metal spoon.

Put a little red jam — slightly less than half a teaspoonful — in the bottom of each barquette case and spread it evenly over the base. Spoon the filling on top of the jam to three-quarters fill each case, and smooth the tops. Bake for 15 to 20 minutes, until the filling is well risen, golden-brown and firm to the touch. Allow the barquettes to cool slightly in their tins, then unmould them on to wire racks to cool fully.

Heat the apricot jam in a small pan until boiling, press it through a nylon sieve to remove any solids, then brush it lightly over each barquette. Arrange chopped cherries and pine-nuts on top of the glaze.

EDITOR'S NOTE: *These barquettes may be stored in an airtight container for two to three days. Toast pine-nuts in a 180°C (350°F or Mark 4) oven for 4 to 5 minutes, until golden; toss the nuts after 2 to 3 minutes so that they colour evenly.*

Honey and Hazelnut Tartlets

Makes 10 tartlets
Working time: about 25 minutes
Total time: about 1 hour and 5 minutes

Per tartlet:
Calories **102**
Protein **2g**
Cholesterol **10mg**
Total fat **11g**
Saturated fat **2g**
Sodium **70mg**

150 g	shortcrust dough (recipe, page 10)	5 oz
60 g	caster sugar	2 oz
2 tbsp	clear honey	2 tbsp
30 g	unsalted butter	1 oz
125 g	shelled hazelnuts, toasted and skinned (box, below)	4 oz

Roll out the dough on a lightly floured surface to a thickness of 3 mm (⅛ inch). Using a 7.5 cm (3 inch) cutter, cut out 10 circles and use these to line 6 cm (2½ inch) tartlet tins. Prick the insides with a fork, set on a baking sheet and chill for 30 minutes. Meanwhile, preheat the oven to 220°C (425°F or Mark 7).

Bake the pastry cases for 15 to 20 minutes, until they are golden-brown. Remove them from the oven, allow to cool a little in the tins, then unmould the tartlet cases on to a wire rack.

To make the filling, place the sugar, honey and 1 tablespoon of water in a small, heavy-bottomed saucepan over low heat. Stir until all the sugar has completely dissolved; if any sugar crystals have stuck to the sides of the pan, brush them down with a pastry brush dipped in warm water. Warm a sugar thermometer in a jug of hot water, then place it in the syrup. Increase the heat to high and bring the syrup to the boil. Boil it rapidly until the temperature on the thermometer registers between 106° and 113°C (223° to 236°F); the syrup will form a fine, short thread when dripped from a spoon. Remove the pan from the heat and stir in the butter and hazelnuts. Spoon the mixture into the pastry cases and leave the tartlets to cool and set before serving.

Skinning Hazelnuts

1 *TOASTING AND SKINNING THE NUTS. Place shelled hazelnuts on a baking sheet in a preheated 180°C (350°F or Mark 4) oven for about 10 minutes. minutes. Lay a towel on a work surface and tip them on to it. Fold the towel over the nuts and, using the palms of your hands, roll the nuts vigorously in the towel. After 1 or 2 minutes, most nuts will have shed their skins.*

2 *REMOVING STUBBORN SKINS. Rub any partly skinned or unskinned nuts between your fingers so that the skin flakes off. Nuts enclosed in their skins even after being rubbed in this way should be reserved for purposes where appearance is not important. Store the nuts in an airtight jar if not using them immediately.*

Rum and Raisin Tartlets

Makes 18 tartlets
Working time: about 35 minutes
Total time: about 6 hours (includes soaking)

Per tartlet:
Calories **125**
Protein **2g**
Cholesterol **25mg**
Total fat **5g**
Saturated fat **1g**
Sodium **45mg**

275 g	shortcrust dough (recipe, page 10)	9 oz
1	orange, rind only, cut into fine shreds with a zester	1
	Rum and raisin filling	
90 g	seedless raisins	3 oz
2 tbsp	white rum	2 tbsp
2	eggs, separated	2
90 g	light brown sugar	3 oz
2 tsp	plain flour	2 tsp
¼ tsp	ground cinnamon	¼ tsp
15 cl	plain low-fat yogurt	¼ pint

First, begin preparations for the filling. Put the raisins and rum into a small saucepan, cover and heat gently for 2 to 3 minutes. Remove the pan from the heat and leave the raisins to soak for at least 4 hours, or preferably overnight.

Roll out the dough on a lightly floured surface to a thickness of 3 mm (⅛ inch). Using a 7.5 cm (3 inch) cutter, cut out 18 circles and use these to line 6 cm (2½ inch) tartlet tins. Prick the insides with a fork and chill them for 30 minutes. Meanwhile, preheat the oven to 200°C (400°F or Mark 6).

Place the tartlet tins on a baking sheet, and bake the cases for about 15 minutes, until crisp and light brown. Remove from the oven and set aside to cool while you complete the filling. Reduce the oven temperature to 180°C (350°F or Mark 4).

In a large bowl, whisk the egg yolks with 60 g (2 oz) of the sugar until thick and pale. In a separate bowl, whisk the egg whites until they form soft peaks, then sprinkle in the remaining sugar and whisk until stiff and glossy. Sift the flour and cinnamon over the beaten egg yolks, add a third of the egg whites and a third of the yogurt and fold all the ingredients in quickly and lightly until the mixture is evenly blended. Add another third of the egg whites and yogurt in the same way, followed by the last third. Fold in the raisins, then fill the tartlet cases with the mixture, making sure that the raisins are evenly distributed.

Bake the tartlets until they are lightly browned and just firm to the touch — 20 to 25 minutes. Transfer the tartlets to a wire rack to cool, and decorate them with shreds of orange rind before serving.

Chocolate Slices

Makes 8 slices
Working time: about 1 hour
Total time: about 3 hours and 30 minutes

Per slice:
Calories **240**
Protein **9g**
Cholesterol **10mg**
Total fat **12g**
Saturated fat **5g**
Sodium **240mg**

125 g	plain flour	4 oz
1 tsp	caster sugar	1 tsp
60 g	polyunsaturated margarine, chilled	2 oz
15 g	cocoa powder	½ oz
3	egg whites	3
250 g	low-fat soft cheese	8 oz
125 g	thick Greek yogurt	4 oz
2 tbsp	clear honey	2 tbsp
2 tsp	powdered gelatine	2 tsp
100 g	plain chocolate	3½ oz

To make the pastry, sift the flour and sugar into a mixing bowl, then rub in the margarine with your fingertips until the mixture resembles fine breadcrumbs. Stir in the cocoa powder and one of the egg whites and mix with a round-bladed knife to form a dough. Gather the dough into a ball and knead it briefly on a lightly floured surface until smooth.

Roll out the dough to a thickness of 3 mm (⅛ inch) and use it to line the base of a 15 cm (6 inch) square loose-based tin that is at least 4 cm (1½ inches) deep. Press the dough well into the corners, prick it all over with a fork, then chill for 30 minutes. Meanwhile, preheat the oven to 220°C (425°F or Mark 7).

Bake the pastry for 15 to 20 minutes until crisp and brown, then remove it from the oven and leave it to cool in the tin while you prepare the filling.

To make the filling, place the cheese, yogurt and 1 tablespoon of the honey in a mixing bowl. Whisk until evenly combined. Sprinkle the gelatine over 2 tablespoons of water in a small bowl and leave it to soften for 2 minutes. Set the bowl over a saucepan of gently simmering water and stir until the gelatine has completely dissolved. Gradually pour the dissolved gelatine into the low-fat cheese, beating well.

Break up the chocolate and reserve a quarter of it. Place the remainder in a bowl set over a saucepan of hot but not boiling water, and leave until melted. Divide the cheese mixture between two bowls. Beat the melted chocolate into one bowl, and beat the remaining tablespoon of honey into the other. In another bowl, whisk the 2 remaining egg whites until they form soft peaks and, using a tablespoon, fold half into the chocolate mixture and half into the honey mixture.

Line the sides of the tin with non-stick parchment paper. Spoon the chocolate mixture over the base and level the surface. Spread the honey mixture over the top, then chill until firm — about 2 hours.

When the filling has set, mark the surface into eight sections. Melt the reserved chocolate as above, and place it in a greaseproof paper piping bag, folded as shown on page 13. Pipe decorative designs over the individual marked sections.

Before serving, carefully lift the whole assembly out of the tin, peel off the paper, and cut into eight slices.

Blackberry and Almond Boats

Makes 16 boats
Working time: about 40 minutes
Total time: about 1 hour and 35 minutes

Per boat:
Calories **150**
Protein **2g**
Cholesterol **trace**
Total fat **7g**
Saturated fat **1g**
Sodium **55mg**

275 g	shortcrust dough (recipe, page 10)	9 oz
2 tsp	icing sugar	2 tsp
Blackberry filling		
250 g	fresh blackberries	8 oz
1 tbsp	arrowroot	1 tbsp
30 g	caster sugar	1 oz
Almond topping		
2	egg whites	2
90 g	vanilla sugar	3 oz
90 g	ground almonds	3 oz

First, prepare the filling. Press the blackberries through a nylon sieve into a non-reactive saucepan. Blend the arrowroot with 1 tablespoon of cold water, and stir into the puréed blackberries. Bring to the boil, stirring continuously; boil until the mixture thickens and clears. Continue to cook over low heat for 3 to 4 minutes, until there is no taste of uncooked arrowroot. Stir in the caster sugar, then leave the purée to cool for about 20 minutes while you roll out the dough.

Preheat the oven to 220°C (425°F or Mark 7). Roll out the dough on a lightly floured surface to a thickness of about 3 mm (⅛ inch). Cut the dough into sixteen 12 by 7 cm (5 by 2¾ inch) rectangles, and use these to line 10 by 4.5 cm (4 by 1¾ inch) fluted barquette tins, pressing the dough well into the flutes. Trim the edges and place the tins on a baking sheet. Divide the cooled fruit purée equally between the lined tins, spreading it evenly.

For the almond topping, whisk the egg whites until you have a froth of small, uniform bubbles, then whisk in the vanilla sugar. Fold in the almonds with a metal spoon. Put the mixture into a piping bag fitted with a 5 mm (¼ inch) plain nozzle. Pipe the almond mixture evenly to cover the surface of the blackberry purée.

Bake the tarts for 20 to 25 minutes, until the topping is well risen and golden-brown; they will probably develop a slight crack in the centre. Allow the tarts to cool in their tins for about 5 minutes, then carefully turn them out on to a wire rack. When the tarts are cool, sift icing sugar very lightly over them.

SUGGESTED ACCOMPANIMENT: *fresh blackberries.*

Souffléed Coffee Diamonds

Makes 10 diamonds
Working time: about 40 minutes
Total time: about 3 hours (includes chilling)

Per diamond:
Calories **170**
Protein **3g**
Cholesterol **30mg**
Total fat **11g**
Saturated fat **4g**
Sodium **100mg**

175 g	plain flour	6 oz
90 g	polyunsaturated margarine, chilled	3 oz
2 tbsp	dark brown sugar	2 tbsp
½ tbsp	cocoa powder	½ tbsp
	Coffee soufflé	
1	egg yolk	1
45 g	light brown sugar	1½ oz
3 tbsp	strong black coffee	3 tbsp
1 tsp	powdered gelatine	1 tsp
2	egg whites	2
8 cl	whipping cream	3 fl oz

To make the diamond cases, sift the flour into a mixing bowl. Rub in the margarine with your fingertips until the mixture resembles fine breadcrumbs, then stir in the sugar. Add 2 teaspoons of cold water and mix to a firm dough with a round-bladed knife. Gather the dough into a ball and knead it briefly on a lightly floured surface until smooth.

Roll out the dough to a thickness of 3 mm (⅛ inch) and, using a sharp knife, cut out ten 11 by 8.5 cm (4½ by 3½ inch) diamonds. Use these to line 8.5 by 6 cm (3½ by 2½ inch) diamond-shaped tartlet tins, pressing the dough firmly into the contours of the tin. Prick the insides with a fork, then put the tartlet tins on a baking sheet and chill for 30 minutes. Meanwhile, re-roll the trimmings, and cut out 30 small leaves. Using the tip of a sharp knife, etch a leaf pattern on to each surface. Place the leaves on a baking sheet and chill with the cases. Preheat the oven to 220°C (425°F or Mark 7).

Bake the leaves for about 3 minutes and the diamond cases for 15 to 20 minutes, until crisp and lightly browned. Allow the cases to cool slightly in their tins, then unmould them on to a wire rack, together with the leaves, to finish cooling.

To make the soufflé, whisk the egg yolk, sugar and coffee in a bowl until pale and frothy — about 5 minutes. Sprinkle the gelatine over 2 tablespoons of water in a small bowl, leave to soften for 2 minutes, then place over a saucepan of gently simmering water, and stir until the gelatine has completely dissolved. Gradually pour it into the coffee mixture, beating well.

Chill the mixture until it has almost set — about 30 minutes. Whisk the two egg whites until stiff, and whip the cream until it holds soft peaks. Using a tablespoon, fold the cream, then the egg whites, into the coffee mixture. Chill again until lightly set — about 1 hour.

Spoon the soufflé into a piping bag fitted with a large star nozzle, and pipe swirls into the cases. Sprinkle with the cocoa powder and decorate with the leaves. Chill for at least 30 minutes before serving.

Chocolate Choux Buns with Strawberry Mousse

Makes 12 buns
Working time: about 30 minutes
Total time: about 1 hour and 30 minutes

Per bun:
Calories **125**
Protein **8g**
Cholesterol **50mg**
Total fat **10g**
Saturated fat **4g**
Sodium **25mg**

	choux dough (recipe, page 10), substituting 15 g (½ oz) of cocoa powder for 15 g (½ oz) of the flour	
1 tbsp	icing sugar	1 tbsp
Strawberry mousse		
2 tsp	powdered gelatine	2 tsp
350 g	strawberries, hulled	12 oz
250 g	fromage frais	8 oz
1 tbsp	caster sugar	1 tbsp
1 tsp	kirsch or eau-de-vie framboise	1 tsp

Preheat the oven to 220°C (425°F or Mark 7).

To make the mousse, first prepare the gelatine by sprinkling it over 2 tablespoons of water in a small bowl and leaving it to soften for 2 minutes. Meanwhile, process 250 g (8 oz) of the strawberries in a food pro-cessor or blender with the *fromage frais*, sugar and kirsch. Place the bowl of gelatine over a pan of sim-mering water and stir until the gelatine has dissolved. Add the dissolved gelatine to the strawberry mixture and process for a further 20 seconds. Then transfer the mousse mixture to a bowl and refrigerate until set – about 1 hour.

Meanwhile, line a baking sheet with non-stick parch-ment paper and drop 12 rounded tablespoons of the prepared dough on to it, spaced well apart, to make buns. Bake for 25 to 30 minutes, until the choux is well risen and firm. Using the tip of a sharp knife, pierce a few small holes in the sides of each bun to allow the steam to escape. Return the buns to the oven for a further 5 minutes to dry out, then transfer them to a wire rack to cool.

Slice the choux buns in half, remove any uncooked dough from the centres, then pipe or spoon the set mousse into the bases. Finely slice the remaining strawberries and arrange the slices on top of the mousse. Replace the bun tops, lightly dust with icing sugar and serve. The buns will hold the filling for about 2 hours before they start to go soft.

Raspberry-Almond Choux Rings on Shortcrust

Makes 28 rings
Working time: about 50 minutes
Total time: about 1 hour and 15 minutes

Per ring:
Calories **90**
Protein **2g**
Cholesterol **40mg**
Total fat **6g**
Saturated fat **2g**
Sodium **60mg**

275 g	shortcrust dough (recipe, page 10)	9 oz
60 g	sliced almonds	2 oz
45 cl	orange-flavoured pastry cream (recipe, page 11)	¾ pint
350 g	fresh raspberries	12 oz
1 tbsp	icing sugar	1 tbsp
Choux dough		
45 g	unsalted butter	1½ oz
60 g	plain flour	2 oz
1	egg	1
1	egg white	1

Roll out the shortcrust dough on a lightly floured sur-face to a thickness of 3 mm (⅛ inch). Prick it well with a fork. Using a 7.5 cm (3 inch) plain cutter, cut out rounds from the dough and place them on baking sheets. Re-roll the trimmings and stamp out more rounds until you have 28 in all. Refrigerate the rounds while making the choux dough.

Preheat the oven to 200°C (400°F or Mark 6).

Make the choux dough according to the method on page 10, using 12.5 cl (4 fl oz) of water and the in-gredients listed above. Transfer the dough to a piping bag fitted with a 5 mm (¼ inch) plain nozzle. Pipe a ring of choux on to each chilled shortcrust round, about 3

mm (⅛ inch) in from the edge. Arrange the almonds evenly over the choux. Bake the rings for 15 to 20 minutes, until the choux is well risen, golden-brown and crisp. Remove the pastries to wire racks to cool.

Fill the centres with the orange-flavoured pastry cream and top the filling with the raspberries. Sift the icing sugar lightly over the finished rings.

EDITOR'S NOTE: *Small strawberries, blackberries, redcurrants or blackcurrants can be substituted for the raspberries.*

Peach Choux Puffs

TRAPPING STEAM TO COOK THE CHOUX PRODUCES A
VERY LARGE, CRISP-TOPPED BUN FROM ONLY A SMALL
AMOUNT OF DOUGH.

Makes 4 puffs
Working time: about 35 minutes
Total time: about 3 hours and 15 minutes (includes chilling)

Per puff:
Calories **150**
Protein **5g**
Cholesterol **75mg**
Total fat **9g**
Saturated fat **4g**
Sodium **25mg**

15 cl	unsweetened orange juice	¼ pint
1 tsp	powdered gelatine	1 tsp
2 tsp	orange-flavoured liqueur (optional)	2 tsp
1	large peach	1
60 g	fromage frais	2 oz
Choux dough		
30 g	unsalted butter	1 oz
45 g	plain flour	1½ oz
1	egg	1

First, make the jelly for the peach filling. Put 1 tablespoon of the orange juice into a small bowl, sprinkle on the gelatine and allow it to soften for 2 minutes. Set the bowl over a pan of gently simmering water and stir until the gelatine has fully dissolved. Stir the gelatine mixture, and the liqueur if using, into the rest of the orange juice in a mixing bowl. Chill until just beginning to set — about 1 hour — while you prepare and cook the choux dough.

Preheat the oven to 220°C (425°F or Mark 7). Grease a baking sheet and find two 1 kg (2 lb) loaf tins, or similar tins, that will sit flat and give a good seal when inverted on to the baking sheet.

Following the method on page 10, make the choux dough with 5 tablespoons of water and the ingredients listed above. Divide the dough into four equal portions, and place them on the baking sheet, positioned so that each loaf tin can cover two buns. Set the loaf tins over the buns and bake them for 35 to 40 minutes, or until the buns move on the baking sheet when the covering tin is gently shaken. Carefully remove the covering tins and transfer the buns to a wire rack to cool.

Skin the peach by dipping it briefly into a bowl of boiling water and then into a bowl of cold water; the skin should slip off easily. Chop the peach flesh roughly, add it to the partially set jelly, then chill again until firmly set — about 2 hours.

Just before serving, assemble the puffs. Cut the tops off the buns and divide the jellied peaches among the bases. Top the peaches with a teaspoon of *fromage frais* and replace the lids.

Tricorn Puffs

Makes 14 puffs
Working time: about 50 minutes
Total time: about 1 hour and 50 minutes

Per puff:
Calories **160**
Protein **5g**
Cholesterol **75mg**
Total fat **8g**
Saturated fat **4g**
Sodium **50mg**

	choux dough (recipe, page 10)	
30 cl	pastry cream (recipe, page 11)	½ pint
250 g	seedless green or black grapes, or a mixture of both, stemmed	8 oz
2 tbsp	apricot jam or orange marmalade	2 tbsp
60 g	shelled almonds, blanched, slivered and toasted	2 oz

Preheat the oven to 220°C (425°F or Mark 7). Line three baking sheets with non-stick parchment paper.

Place the choux dough in a piping bag fitted with a 1.5 cm (⅝ inch) plain nozzle. Pipe 14 "tricorns" on to the prepared baking sheets by piping three balls of dough for each one, with the balls touching to make a triangle shape. Bake the tricorns for 25 to 30 minutes, or until the pastry is well risen, golden-brown and crisp. Remove the tricorn puffs from the oven and, with the tip of a sharp knife, pierce a small hole in the side of each. Return the tricorns to the oven for a further 5 minutes to dry them out, then transfer them to wire racks to cool.

Split the puffs in half and remove any uncooked dough from the centres. Fill the bases with the pastry cream and a few grapes; if the grapes are large, halve or quarter them first. Replace the tricorn tops. Heat the jam or marmalade in a small saucepan until liquid, sieve it to remove any solids, then use a pastry brush to paint a little over the top of each puff. Sprinkle on a few toasted almond slivers and serve within 1 hour.

EDITOR'S NOTE: *To blanch almonds, put them in boiling water for 1 minute, drain them thoroughly, then use your fingers to pop them out of their skins. To toast slivered almonds put them under the grill for 2 minutes, or until they become golden; turn or shake them constantly.*

Fresh Fruit Galette

Makes 16 slices
Working time: about 1 hour and 40 minutes
Total time: about 3 hours and 15 minutes (includes chilling)

Per slice:
Calories **220**
Protein **4g**
Cholesterol **50mg**
Total fat **8g**
Saturated fat **4g**
Sodium **75mg**

30 cl	liqueur-flavoured pastry cream (recipe, page 11), using Cointreau or other orange-flavoured liqueur, made with one egg yolk instead of two	½ pint
175 g	strawberries, hulled and sliced	6 oz
2	kiwi fruit, peeled, halved lengthwise and sliced	2
350 g	fresh pineapple, skinned, quartered, cored and sliced	12 oz
12	black grapes, halved and pips removed	12
2	large peaches, skinned, halved, stoned and sliced	2
2 tsp	icing sugar	2 tsp
15 cl	white wine	¼ pint
60 g	caster sugar	2 oz
2 tbsp	Cointreau or other orange-flavoured liqueur	2 tbsp
Rich shortcrust base		
150 g	plain flour	5 oz
15 g	icing sugar	½ oz
75 g	unsalted butter, chilled	2½ oz
1	egg yolk, lightly beaten	1
	a little beaten egg white for brushing	
Choux dough		
45 g	unsalted butter	1½ oz
60 g	plain flour	2 oz
1	egg	1
1	egg white	1

First make the shortcrust base. Sift the flour and sugar into a mixing bowl. Rub in the butter until the mixture resembles fine breadcrumbs, then make a well in the centre. Add the egg yolk and 5 teaspoons of iced water, and mix with a round-bladed knife to form a fairly stiff dough. Knead the dough very lightly on a floured surface until smooth, then wrap it in plastic film and refrigerate it for 30 minutes.

Roll out the dough on a lightly floured surface into a square a little larger than 30 cm (12 inches). Trim the square to exactly 30 cm (12 inches). Prick the dough well with a fork and cut it in half to make two equal rectangles. Place the rectangles on one large or two small baking sheets. Refrigerate them for 30 minutes.

Preheat the oven to 200°C (400°F or Mark 6). Prepare the choux dough according to the method on page 10, using 12.5 cl (4 fl oz) of water and the ingredients listed above. Put the dough into a piping bag fitted with a 1 cm (½ inch) 12-point star nozzle. Brush a 1 cm (½ inch) wide strip of beaten egg white down each long side of the chilled rectangles of shortcrust. Carefully pipe an even, single line of choux on top of the egg white, about 5 mm (¼ inch) in from the edge.

Bake the doughs until the choux is well risen, golden-brown and firm to the touch — about 25 minutes. Using the tip of a small, sharp knife, make several incisions along the inside edge of each choux strip, to allow the steam to escape. Return the galette bases to the oven for 5 minutes, then carefully transfer them to wire racks to cool.

Slice the choux strips in half horizontally and scoop out any uncooked dough. Fit a piping bag with a 1 cm (½ inch) 12-point star nozzle and fill it with the pastry cream. Pipe a line of cream filling into each choux strip, and replace the tops. Spread the remaining pastry cream in an even layer over the shortcrust base, between the choux strips. Arrange the prepared fruits in neat lines on top of the pastry cream. Sift the icing sugar lightly over the choux borders.

Finally, make a glaze for the fruit. Put the wine, caster sugar and Cointreau into a small saucepan. Heat gently, stirring, until the sugar dissolves, then boil the syrup for 3 to 4 minutes, until it is reduced and syrupy. Brush the glaze evenly over the fruit.

Cut each galette into eight slices for serving and eat on the day of preparation.

Wholemeal Raspberry Choux

Makes 12 buns
Working time: about 25 minutes
Total time: about 1 hour and 10 minutes

Per bun:
Calories **95**
Protein **3g**
Cholesterol **50mg**
Total fat **6g**
Saturated fat **3g**
Sodium **100mg**

60 g	unsalted butter	2 oz
45 g	wholemeal flour, sifted, bran reserved	1½ oz
30 g	plain flour, sifted	1 oz
2	eggs, lightly beaten	2
1 tsp	sesame seeds	1 tsp
1 tbsp	icing sugar	1 tbsp
Raspberry-cheese filling		
175 g	low-fat curd cheese	6 oz
1 tbsp	clear honey	1 tbsp
125 g	fresh raspberries	4 oz

Preheat the oven to 200°C (400°F or Mark 6). Line a large baking sheet with non-stick parchment paper.

Put the butter and 15 cl (¼ pint) of water into a heavy-bottomed saucepan and heat gently until the butter melts. Increase the heat to medium high and bring the liquid to the boil. Remove the pan from the heat, add the two types of flour and the bran all at once, and beat vigorously with a wooden spoon. Return the pan to the heat and continue beating until the mixture forms a ball in the centre of the pan. Allow the mixture to cool for a few minutes.

Set aside 1 tablespoon of the beaten egg. Using an electric hand-held mixer, beat the remaining egg, a little at a time, into the partly cooled mixture. Continue beating until the dough forms a smooth shiny paste.

Spoon 12 mounds of the choux dough, spaced well apart, on to the prepared baking sheet. Brush them with the reserved beaten egg and sprinkle them with the sesame seeds. Bake until the choux is crisp and golden-brown — 20 to 25 minutes. Using the point of a sharp knife, pierce each bun to allow the steam to escape, then return them to the oven for a further

5 minutes to dry out. Let them cool on a wire rack.

To make the filling, beat together the cheese and honey until smooth, then gently fold in the raspberries. Split the buns horizontally and scoop out any soft dough inside. Spoon some filling on to each bottom half, replace the tops and sift on a little icing sugar.

Orange and Date Choux

Makes 14 buns
Working time: about 1 hour and 15 minutes
Total time: about 2 hours

Per bun:
Calories **160**
Protein **3g**
Cholesterol **50mg**
Total fat **7g**
Saturated fat **5g**
Sodium **20mg**

28	small unblemished rose leaves	28
90 g	plain chocolate	3 oz
	choux dough (recipe, page 10)	
2 tsp	icing sugar	2 tsp
	orange slices (optional)	
Fruit filling		
3	oranges	3
250 g	fresh dates, stoned and roughly chopped	8 oz
⅛ tsp	ground cinnamon	⅛ tsp
2 tsp	icing sugar	2 tsp
125 g	fromage frais	4 oz
6 cl	whipping cream	2 fl oz

First, prepare the chocolate leaves for decoration. Wash and dry the rose leaves thoroughly. Melt the chocolate on a heatproof plate set over a pan of simmering water, stirring gently. Holding each leaf by its stem, gently press the underside of the leaf into the melted chocolate, then pull it across the side of the plate to remove excess chocolate. Place the leaves, chocolate side up, on a clean plate and leave them to set in a cool place — not the refrigerator.

Preheat the oven to 220°C (425°F or Mark 7). Line three baking sheets with non-stick parchment paper and draw on fourteen 6 cm (2½ inch) circles, spaced well apart; turn the papers over.

Spoon the choux dough into a piping bag fitted with a 1 cm (½ inch) plain nozzle. Beginning in the centre of each circle, pipe a continuous spiral of choux dough to fill each circle. Bake the buns for 25 to 30 minutes, or until they are well risen, golden-brown and crisp. Remove the choux from the oven, pierce a hole in the side of each with the tip of a sharp knife, then return them to the oven for another 5 minutes to dry out the insides. Cool the buns on wire racks.

To make the filling, grate the rind of one orange into a mixing bowl and add the dates. Slice off the rind and pith from all three oranges and cut them into segments (box, opposite page). Cut each segment into two or three pieces, and add them to the mixing bowl. Mix the cinnamon and icing sugar into the *fromage frais*, then gently fold this into the date and orange mixture. Whip the cream until stiff, and place it in a piping bag fitted with a 1 cm (½ inch) star nozzle.

Cut a lid from the top of each bun, and remove any uncooked dough from the inside. Spoon the date and orange filling into the bases, and replace the lids. Sift the icing sugar over the buns, then pipe a whirl of cream on top of each one.

Starting from the stem end, carefully peel off the green rose leaves from their chocolate coating and arrange two chocolate leaves in every cream whirl. Serve accompanied by slices of orange, if liked.

Segmenting an Orange

1 REMOVING THE PEEL. Using a sharp knife, slice off the peel at both ends of the orange. Stand the fruit on a flat end and slice downwards to remove the rind and pith in vertical strips. This technique of cutting away rind and pith together ensures that every trace of pith is removed.

2 CUTTING OUT THE SEGMENTS. Working over a bowl to catch the juice, hold the orange in one hand and slice between flesh and membrane to remove each segment. The segments will now make a fresh and appealing filling or decoration.

Pear and Hazelnut Choux Buns

Makes 36 buns
Working time: about 1 hour
Total time: about 1 hour and 30 minutes

Per bun:
Calories **75**
Protein **2g**
Cholesterol **20mg**
Total fat **5g**
Saturated fat **2g**
Sodium **30mg**

35 g	shelled hazelnuts, toasted and skinned (page 29), finely chopped	1¼ oz
	choux dough (recipe, page 10)	
8	large ripe firm pears	8
1 tsp	fresh lemon juice	1 tsp
15 g	unsalted butter	½ oz
30 g	caster sugar	1 oz
1½ tbsp	icing sugar	1½ tbsp

Preheat the oven to 220°C (425°F or Mark 7). Line two large baking sheets with non-stick parchment paper.

Reserve 1 tablespoon of chopped hazelnuts; stir the remainder into the freshly prepared choux dough. Spoon the dough into a piping bag fitted with a 2 cm (¾ inch) plain nozzle. Spacing them well apart, pipe 36 small rounds of choux, about 4 cm (1½ inches) in diameter, on to the prepared sheets. Top them with the reserved hazelnuts, pressing the nuts gently into the dough, then bake until the buns are crisp and golden-brown on both the top and sides — 20 to 25 minutes. Using the point of a sharp knife, pierce each bun to allow the steam to escape, then return them to the oven for a further 5 minutes to dry out thoroughly. Let the buns cool on a wire rack.

While the buns are baking, peel, core and thinly slice the pears. Put the slices into a non-reactive saucepan with the lemon juice and 2 teaspoons of water and cook over moderate heat, stirring occasionally, until the mixture is reduced to a soft purée. Increase the heat and cook until the mixture is nearly dry. Stir in the butter and caster sugar and continue to cook over a high heat until the mixture begins to brown. Drain off any remaining liquid and set the mixture aside to cool.

Just before serving, slit the buns in half horizontally and spoon the pear filling into the bottom halves. Replace the tops and sift on the icing sugar.

Caramel-Topped Apple Choux Fingers

Makes 20 fingers
Working time: about 1 hour
Total time: about 1 hour and 30 minutes

Per finger:
Calories **70**
Protein **1g**
Cholesterol **35mg**
Total fat **4g**
Saturated fat **2g**
Sodium **15mg**

	choux dough (recipe, page 10)	
4	dessert apples	4
1 tsp	calvados	1 tsp
2 tbsp	thick Greek yogurt	2 tbsp
90 g	caster sugar	3 oz

Preheat the oven to 220°C (425°F or Mark 7). Line a large baking sheet with non-stick parchment paper.

Spoon the choux dough into a piping bag fitted with a 1 cm (½ inch) plain nozzle. Pipe twenty 7.5 cm (3 inch) choux fingers, spaced well apart, on to the prepared sheet, cutting the dough off with a wet knife when the required length is reached. Bake the fingers until the pastry is well risen and golden-brown — 25 to 30 minutes. Using the tip of a sharp knife, pierce a few small holes in each finger to allow the steam to escape, then bake for a further 5 minutes to dry them out thoroughly. Cool the fingers on a wire rack.

While the fingers are baking, make the filling. Peel, core and thinly slice the apples into a heavy-bottomed saucepan with 1 tablespoon of water. Cook them over a low heat, covered, until they become soft and the liquid has evaporated. Allow to cool — about 30 minutes — then stir in the calvados and yogurt.

To make the caramel topping, put the sugar and 2 tablespoons of water into a small, heavy-bottomed saucepan placed over low heat, and allow the sugar to dissolve without stirring. Warm a sugar thermometer in a jug of hot water, then place it in the pan. Bring the syrup to the boil and cook it rapidly until it turns a rich brown colour — the temperature on the thermometer should be between 160° and 170°C (320° and 338°F). Brush down any sugar crystals stuck to the sides of the pan with a bristle pastry brush dipped in hot water (a nylon brush will disintegrate in the heat).

Remove the pan from the heat and place it, briefly, in a large pan of cold water to arrest cooking, then set it in hot water to keep the caramel fluid. Holding the choux fingers very carefully, dip them in the hot caramel to coat their tops. Place the coated fingers, caramel side up, on a wire rack set over greaseproof paper and allow the topping to set — about 5 minutes. Cut the choux fingers in half horizontally and spoon in a little of the apple mixture. Serve immediately.

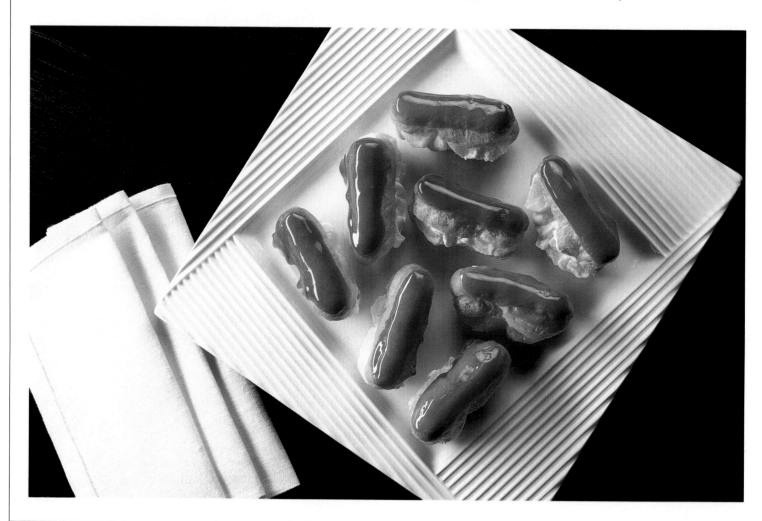

Mango and Ginger Choux Buns

Makes 24 buns
Working time: about 45 minutes
Total time: about 1 hour and 20 minutes

Per bun:		choux dough (recipe, page 10)	
Calories **100**	17.5 cl	whipping cream	6 fl oz
Protein **2g**	2	ripe mangoes, peeled, stoned	2
Cholesterol **30mg**		and diced	
Total fat **5g**			
Saturated fat **3g**	125 g	icing sugar, sifted	4 oz
Sodium **40mg**	1 tsp	ground ginger	1 tsp

Preheat the oven to 220°C (425°F or Mark 7). Line two large baking sheets with non-stick parchment paper.

Spoon the choux dough into a piping bag fitted with a 1 cm (½ inch) plain nozzle. Pipe twenty-four 7.5 cm (3 inch) rings of dough, spaced well apart, on to the prepared sheet; keep the hole in the centre of each ring as small as possible as you pipe — when baked, the rings will close up and form buns. Bake the rings until they are well risen and golden-brown — 25 to 30 minutes. Using the tip of a sharp knife, pierce each bun two or three times, to allow steam to escape. Return them to the oven for a further 5 minutes to dry out thoroughly, then cool them on a wire rack.

When the buns are cool, split them horizontally with a sharp knife and remove any uncooked dough from inside. Whip the cream until stiff, then transfer it to a piping bag fitted with a 5 mm (¼ inch) star nozzle. Pipe a circle of cream round the edge of the lower half of each bun, spoon diced mango into the centre, then replace the top halves of the buns.

Beat the icing sugar and ginger with 2 teaspoons of water until the mixture is smooth and glossy. Fold a greaseproof paper piping bag (page 13) and fill it with the icing. Snip off the tip of the bag and dribble a zig-zag pattern over the tops of the buns.

Wine Choux Éclairs

Makes 20 éclairs
Working time: about 1 hour
Total time: about 3 hours

Per éclair:
Calories **75**
Protein **1g**
Cholesterol **15mg**
Total fat **3g**
Saturated fat **2g**
Sodium **30mg**

1	large orange	1
1	lemon	1
30 cl	white wine	½ pint
60 g	caster sugar	2 oz
30 g	cornflour	1 oz
2 tbsp	double cream	2 tbsp
60 g	icing sugar	2 oz
Choux dough		
12.5 cl	white wine	4 fl oz
45 g	unsalted butter	1½ oz
60 g	plain flour	2 oz
1	whole egg	1
1	egg white	1

Begin by preparing the filling and decoration. Using a vegetable peeler, thinly pare the rind from the orange and the lemon, cutting long strips from the top to the bottom. Cut one third of the strips into fine shreds and set them aside. Put the remaining strips into a non-reactive saucepan with the wine. Bring the wine just to the point of boiling, then remove the saucepan from the heat. Cover it and leave the mixture to stand for at least 30 minutes.

Meanwhile, put 30 g (1 oz) of the caster sugar into a small saucepan with 2 tablespoons of cold water. Heat gently until the sugar dissolves, then bring the mixture to the boil. Add the finely shredded orange and lemon rind and cook gently for 1 minute, until the shreds soften. Pour the shreds into a nylon sieve to drain; discard the sugar syrup. Line a small tray with non-stick parchment paper. Separate the shreds and place them individually on the paper, then set aside to dry.

Using a slotted spoon, remove the strips of orange and lemon rind from the wine and discard them. In a small bowl, blend the cornflour with a little of the wine to make a smooth cream. Stir the cornflour mixture and the remaining caster sugar into the wine in the saucepan. Bring to the boil over a moderate heat, stirring constantly until the mixture thickens and clears. Continue to cook over low heat for 2 to 3 minutes, until no taste of raw cornflour remains. Remove the saucepan from the heat and cover the surface of the mixture with plastic film, to prevent a skin forming. Allow it to cool — about 20 minutes.

Whip the cream until it forms soft peaks. When the wine mixture is cool, whisk it until smooth, then gradually fold in the cream. Re-cover the surface of the wine cream with plastic film and refrigerate while making the éclairs.

Preheat the oven to 220°C (425°F or Mark 7). Line one large baking sheet, or two small ones, with non-stick parchment paper.

Prepare the choux dough as directed on page 10, using the ingredients listed above — here, wine replaces the water. Put the choux dough into a piping bag fitted with a 1 cm (½ inch) star nozzle. Pipe twenty 7.5 cm (3 inch) lengths of choux, spaced well apart, on to the lined baking sheet, cutting the dough off with a small knife at the correct length. Bake the éclairs until they are well risen and golden-brown — 20 to 25 minutes. Pierce each éclair with the tip of a small knife, to allow the steam to escape, then return them to the oven for a further 5 minutes to dry out. Transfer the éclairs to a wire rack to cool.

Using a sharp knife, cut each éclair in half horizontally. Pipe or spoon the wine cream into the base of each one and replace the top.

Sift the icing sugar into a small bowl and blend it with 3 teaspoons of boiling water to make a smooth glacé icing. Using a pastry brush, brush the icing over the top of the éclairs, then decorate them with the orange and lemon shreds. Set the éclairs aside in a cool place until the icing sets — 20 to 30 minutes. Eat them the day they are made.

Mini Paris-Brest

THE FIRST PARIS-BREST WAS NAMED BY A TURN-OF-THE-
CENTURY FRENCH PATISSIER IN HONOUR OF THE FAMOUS
BICYCLE RACE OF THE SAME NAME. RING-SHAPED TO RESEMBLE
A WHEEL, IT WAS TRADITIONALLY FILLED WITH AN ALMOND
PRALINE PASTRY CREAM. HERE, THE CREAM IS LIGHTENED WITH
YOGURT, AND HAZELNUTS — WHICH ARE LESS FATTY THAN
ALMONDS — ARE USED IN THE PRALINE.

Makes 20 rings
Working time: about 1 hour
Total time: about 2 hours

Per ring:
Calories **100**
Protein **2g**
Cholesterol **35mg**
Total fat **7g**
Saturated fat **4g**
Sodium **20mg**

	choux dough (page 10)	
90 g	shelled hazelnuts, toasted and skinned (page 29)	3 oz
90 g	caster sugar	3 oz
4 tbsp	double cream	4 tbsp
30 cl	thick Greek yogurt	½ pint
1 tbsp	icing sugar	1 tbsp
3	glacé cherries, thinly sliced	3

Preheat the oven to 220°C (425°F or Mark 7). Line two baking sheets with non-stick parchment paper, then draw 20 circles on the baking paper, using a 6 cm (2½ inch) plain cutter as a guide. Invert the paper so that the pencil marks face downwards.

Spoon the choux dough into a piping bag fitted with a 1 cm (½ inch) star nozzle. Following the drawn circles, pipe rings of choux on to the parchment paper. Bake them until they are well risen, golden-brown and firm to the touch — 20 to 25 minutes. Using the point of a sharp knife, pierce each choux ring in several places round the outside to allow the steam to escape, then return them to the oven for 5 minutes to dry out completely. Let them cool on wire racks. As soon as the rings are cool, cut each one in half horizontally and scoop out any uncooked choux. Keep the rings in their matching pairs.

Lightly butter a small baking sheet for the praline. Put the hazelnuts and sugar into a small, heavy-bottomed saucepan and stir over a low heat until the sugar dissolves and turns to a golden caramel colour. Immediately the nut mixture turns to caramel, pour it on to the buttered sheet. Leave it in a cool place until it has set hard — about 30 minutes.

Break the hardened praline into pieces and put them in a strong plastic bag placed inside another. Crush the praline to a fine powder with a mallet or a wooden rolling pin. Pass the praline through a coarse-meshed metal sieve and return any large pieces to the bag for further crushing.

Whip the cream until it is thick but not buttery. Gently mix in the yogurt, then fold in the hazelnut praline, reserving 1 tablespoon for decoration.

Spoon a little praline cream into the bottom half of each choux ring, then replace the tops. Sift icing sugar lightly over the rings, and decorate them with cherry slices and a sprinkling of the reserved praline.

Chocolate-Caramel Éclairs

Makes 24 éclairs
Working time: about 50 minutes
Total time: about 1 hour and 50 minutes

Per éclair:
Calories **75**
Protein **1g**
Cholesterol **30mg**
Total fat **4g**
Saturated fat **2g**
Sodium **10mg**

	choux dough (recipe, page 10)	
175 g	granulated sugar	6 oz
30 g	shelled pistachio nuts, skinned and chopped	1 oz
60 cl	chocolate-flavoured pastry cream (recipe, page 11)	1 pint

Preheat the oven to 220°C (425°F or Mark 7). Line two large baking sheets with non-stick parchment paper.

Spoon the choux dough into a piping bag fitted with a 1 cm (½ inch) plain nozzle. Pipe twenty-four 7.5 cm (3 inch) lengths of choux, spaced well apart, on to the prepared baking sheets, cutting the mixture off at the nozzle with a wet knife at the correct length. Bake until the pastry is well risen, golden-brown and crisp — 25 to 30 minutes. Using the point of a sharp knife, pierce a small hole in one end of each éclair. Return them to the oven for 5 minutes to dry out completely. Let them cool on wire racks.

To make the caramel, put the sugar into a small, heavy-bottomed saucepan with 8 cl (3 fl oz) of water and stir over gentle heat until the sugar has dissolved. Brush down any sugar crystals stuck to the sides of the pan with a bristle pastry brush dipped in hot water (a nylon brush will disintegrate in the heat). Warm a sugar thermometer in a jug of hot water, then place it in the pan. Boil rapidly until the thermometer registers between 160° and 170°C (320° and 338°F); the syrup will have turned a light golden-brown. Remove the pan from the heat and place it, briefly, in a large pan of cold water to arrest the cooking, then in hot water to keep the caramel fluid. Holding each éclair carefully with your fingers, dip the top into the caramel. Sprinkle immediately with pistachio nuts and place on a wire rack set over a sheet of greaseproof paper. Leave the éclairs until the caramel hardens — about 5 minutes.

Put the pastry cream into a piping bag fitted with a 1 cm (½ inch) star nozzle. Slit each éclair along one side, just under the caramel topping, open them out and fill them with pastry cream.

Serve the éclairs within 2 to 3 hours of filling. Until then, keep them in a cool dry place — a damp or humid atmosphere will make the caramel sticky.

EDITOR'S NOTE: *To skin pistachio nuts, blanch them in boiling water for 1 minute, drain them thoroughly, then rub them vigorously in a towel.*

Phyllo Fans

Makes 16 fans
Working time: about 45 minutes
Total time: about 55 minutes

Per fan:
Calories **80**
Protein **1g**
Cholesterol **15mg**
Total fat **3g**
Saturated fat **1g**
Sodium **20mg**

60 g	ground almonds	2 oz
125 g	plus 1 tbsp light brown sugar	4 oz
2	lemons, grated rind and juice	2
1 tbsp	skimmed milk	1 tbsp
1	egg	1
4	sheets phyllo pastry, each about 45 by 30 cm (18 by 12 inches)	4
1 tsp	safflower oil	1 tsp
30 g	plain chocolate	1 oz

Place the ground almonds in a mixing bowl with the tablespoon of sugar, lemon rind and skimmed milk. Add the egg and beat the mixture to a smooth paste.

In a small, heavy-bottomed saucepan, make a lemon glaze by gently heating the lemon juice with the remaining sugar. Stir until the sugar has dissolved, then bring the mixture to the boil and cook it until it is syrupy — about 2 minutes. Set the glaze aside to cool.

Preheat the oven to 200°C (400°F or Mark 6). Place the sheets of phyllo in a pile and keep them covered with a clean, damp cloth.

Lay one sheet of phyllo on a work surface and spread it evenly with half the almond mixture. Cover this with another sheet of phyllo and press it down lightly. Cut the sheets in half widthwise, then into four lengthwise, to form eight small filled strips, each 22.5 by 7.5 cm (9 by 3 inches).

Starting from the short edge of one strip, fold it into eight to 10 even pleats. Transfer the pleated strip to a baking sheet and, pinching the pleats together at one end, open out the other end into a fan shape. Repeat with the other strips, then use the remaining filling and pastry to make eight more fans. Brush the fans lightly with the oil and bake them until they are deep gold — 7 to 8 minutes. Remove from the oven and brush with the lemon glaze. Set them aside to cool.

Break the chocolate into a heatproof bowl set over a pan of hot, but not boiling, water. Stir gently until the chocolate has melted, then fill a small greaseproof paper piping bag *(page 13)* with the melted chocolate. Cut a small hole at the tip of the bag and decorate the fans with fine chocolate piping.

Phyllo Pastry Fruits

Makes 12 pastry fruits
Working time: about 30 minutes
Total time: about 1 hour and 20 minutes

Per fruit:
Calories **50**
Protein **1g**
Cholesterol **10mg**
Total fat **2g**
Saturated fat **1g**
Sodium **15mg**

4	apricots, halved and stoned	4
4	plums, halved and stoned	4
4	figs, peeled and halved	4
4	sheets phyllo pastry, each about 45 by 30 cm (18 by 12 inches)	4
30 g	unsalted butter, melted	1 oz
1 tsp	flaked almonds	1 tsp
	icing sugar, to decorate	
	Rose rice filling	
15 cl	skimmed milk	¼ pint
30 g	ground rice	1 oz
1 tsp	caster sugar	1 tsp
3 tsp	rose-water	3 tsp

To make the filling, put the milk into a small saucepan and bring it to the boil over medium heat. Sprinkle in the ground rice and stir continuously until the mixture comes back to the boil. Reduce the heat and simmer for 2 minutes, then stir in the caster sugar and rose-water, and set aside to cool.

Meanwhile, cut each sheet of phyllo into six 15 cm (6 inch) squares. Stack the 24 squares in a pile and cover with a clean, damp cloth to prevent them drying out, removing them as required.

Spread some of the cooled filling on to the cut faces of each piece of fruit, filling the cavities in the apricots and plums, then sandwich the fruit halves back together again to form whole fruits.

Preheat the oven to 200°C (400°F or Mark 6) while you wrap each fruit in two squares of phyllo as follows. To wrap the apricots, place each fruit on its side at the centre of one edge of a phyllo square and roll it up. Twist both ends like a cracker, brush with melted butter, then roll the wrapped fruit in a second square of phyllo in the same way. For the plums, place each fruit, stem end up, in the centre of a phyllo square. Gather the pastry up round the fruit and twist it at the top. Brush with melted butter, then wrap the fruit in a second square. Smooth the top edges of pastry down over the fruit. Wrap figs in the same way as plums, but tease open the layers of pastry at the top of the fruit rather than smoothing them flat.

Place the wrapped fruits, spaced well apart, on a lightly buttered baking sheet. Brush a little more melted butter on to each fruit and sprinkle flaked almonds over the apricots. Bake the fruits for about 10 minutes, until they are lightly browned at the edges. Transfer to a wire rack and, as soon as the pastry fruits are cool — about 30 minutes — sift a little icing sugar over each one and serve.

Quince and Chestnut Strudel

Makes 18 slices
Working time: about 1 hour
Total time: about 2 hours and 40 minutes

Per slice:
Calories **235**
Protein **7g**
Cholesterol **15mg**
Total fat **6g**
Saturated fat **4g**
Sodium **190mg**

500 g	fresh quinces	1 lb
125 g	light brown sugar	4 oz
½	lemon, grated rind and juice	½
1	stick cinnamon	1
125 g	chestnuts	4 oz
250 g	low-fat soft cheese	8 oz
1 tsp	ground cinnamon	1 tsp
1 tsp	finely-grated orange rind	1 tsp
3	sheets phyllo pastry, each about 45 by 30 cm (18 by 12 inches)	3
30 g	unsalted butter, melted	1 oz
1 tbsp	icing sugar	1 tbsp

Peel and core the quinces and cut them lengthwise into slices 2 cm (¾ inch) thick, reserving the skins. Place the slices in acidulated water to prevent discoloration. In a non-reactive saucepan, dissolve the brown sugar in 30 cl (½ pint) of water. Add the lemon rind and juice, the cinnamon stick and the quince skins, and simmer for about 20 minutes. Strain the syrup and return it to the pan. Drain the quince slices and poach them in the syrup until they are tender — about 30 minutes. Meanwhile, peel the chestnuts *(box, below)*, simmer them in a saucepan of water for about 20 minutes until tender but unbroken, then drain and chop them roughly.

Using a slotted spoon, transfer the poached quince slices to a plate to cool, reserving 2 tablespoons of the poaching syrup. In a mixing bowl, combine the cheese, reserved syrup, ground cinnamon and orange rind.

Preheat the oven to 190°C (375°F or Mark 5). Lightly grease a baking sheet.

Place a sheet of phyllo on a work surface, keeping the others covered by a clean, damp cloth, and brush the sheet lightly with a little of the melted butter. Fold it in half widthwise to form a 30 by 22.5 cm (12 by 9 inch) rectangle. Spread one third of the cheese mixture down one long side of the phyllo sheet, leaving a 4 cm (1½ inch) margin free of filling along the edge and at each end. Arrange one third of the chestnuts on top of the cheese, and one third of the quince slices on top of the chestnuts. Roll the long edge of the pastry over so as just to enclose the filling. Brush the other three edges of the pastry with more melted butter. Fold the two short edges over the filling and roll up the pastry lengthwise. Place the strudel, seam downwards, on the prepared baking sheet, and brush the top with a little more melted butter. Assemble and roll up two more strudels in the same way.

Bake the three strudels until crisp and golden-brown — 35 to 45 minutes. Cool them on a wire rack, and dust them with a little sifted icing sugar just before slicing and serving.

EDITOR'S NOTE: *Firm pears may be substituted for quinces: they should be poached for 10 minutes only and drained well on paper towels; 2 tablespoons of quince preserve should also be added to the cheese mixture. The unbaked strudels may be frozen and baked when required.*

Peeling Chestnuts

1 *PREPARING THE CHESTNUTS. With a sharp knife, cut a cross in the hull of each chestnut (above). Drop the chestnuts into boiling water and parboil them for about 10 minutes, to loosen their hulls. Remove the pan from the heat.*

2 *PEELING OFF THE SKINS. With a slotted spoon, lift out the chestnuts a few at a time. Peel off the hulls and inner skins while the chestnuts are hot.*

Muesli and Apple Strudel

Serves 12
Working time: about 30 minutes
Total time: about 1 hour and 30 minutes

Calories **60**
Protein **1g**
Cholesterol **trace**
Total fat **2g**
Saturated fat **1g**
Sodium **20mg**

2 tsp	safflower oil	2 tsp
45 g	sugar-free muesli with high fruit and nut content	1 ½ oz
30 g	light brown sugar	1 oz
1 tsp	ground cinnamon	1 tsp
4	sheets phyllo pastry, each about 45 by 30 cm (18 by 12 inches)	4
15 g	unsalted butter, melted	½ oz
350 g	cooking apples, peeled, cored and thinly sliced	12 oz
1 tsp	icing sugar	1 tsp

Preheat the oven to 200°C (400°F or Mark 6).

To make the filling, heat the oil in a small saucepan. Add the muesli and fry it gently for about 2 minutes until crisp. Stir in the light brown sugar and ½ teaspoon of the cinnamon, and set the mixture aside to cool.

Place a sheet of phyllo on a work surface and brush it lightly with melted butter. Lay the remaining sheets over the first, brushing each one with a little melted butter. Arrange the apple slices evenly along one long edge of the phyllo and sprinkle them with the muesli mixture. Starting from the long filled edge, roll up the phyllo, enclosing the filling, and place it, seam down, on a lightly buttered baking sheet. (Bend the strudel into a crescent if the baking sheet is too small.)

Brush the strudel with the remaining melted butter and bake it until the pastry is crisp and golden — about 30 minutes. Cool on a wire rack or serve hot, straight from the oven. Before serving, combine the icing sugar and remaining cinnamon and sift over the top of the strudel. Cut diagonally into 12 slices.

Almond Spirals

Makes 18 spirals
Working time: about 35 minutes
Total time: about 50 minutes

Per spiral:
Calories **85**
Protein **2g**
Cholesterol **trace**
Total fat **6g**
Saturated fat **2g**
Sodium **5mg**

125 g	ground almonds	4 oz
90 g	caster sugar	3 oz
1	egg white	1
¼ tsp	pure almond extract	¼ tsp
6	sheets phyllo pastry, each about 45 by 30 cm (18 by 12 inches)	6
45 g	unsalted butter, melted	1½ oz
	icing sugar, to decorate	

In a mixing bowl, combine the ground almonds, caster sugar, egg white and almond extract to give a smooth paste. Divide the paste into 18 equal portions.

Cut each sheet of phyllo widthwise into three equal rectangles measuring 30 by 15 cm (12 by 6 inches). Stack all 18 rectangles in one pile, then cover them with a clean, damp cloth.

Preheat the oven to 190°C (375°F or Mark 5).

Assemble the spirals one at a time to prevent the phyllo from drying out. Take a portion of almond paste and roll it on a work surface into a 29 cm (11½ inch) long, thin sausage. If the paste sticks, powder the work surface with a little icing sugar. Place a sheet of phyllo on the worktop and brush with a little melted butter, then place the roll of almond paste along one long edge of the pastry. Roll up the phyllo, enclosing the almond filling, then shape the roll into a spiral. Repeat this process until all the portions of almond paste and phyllo rectangles have been made into spirals.

Arrange the phyllo spirals on baking trays, pressing the loose ends against the sides of the trays in order to prevent them from unrolling. Brush each spiral with melted butter, then bake them for 12 to 15 minutes, until golden-brown.

Remove the spirals from the oven and cool them on wire racks. Before serving, sift a little icing sugar over each pastry to decorate.

Poppy Seed Pillows

Makes 16 pillows
Working time: about 35 minutes
Total time: about 1 hour

Per pillow:
Calories **110**
Protein **3g**
Cholesterol **trace**
Total fat **6g**
Saturated fat **1g**
Sodium **25mg**

125 g	plus 1 tsp poppy seeds	4 oz
¼ litre	fresh orange juice	8 fl oz
125 g	sultanas	4 oz
60 g	light brown sugar	2 oz
1	orange, grated rind only	1
⅛ tsp	mixed spice	⅛ tsp
6	sheets phyllo pastry, each about 45 by 30 cm (18 by 12 inches)	6
30 g	unsalted butter, melted	1 oz

Finely grind 125 g (4 oz) of the poppy seeds in a coffee grinder and place them in a saucepan with the orange juice. (Alternatively, blend the seeds and juice in a food processor or blender.) Stir in the sultanas, sugar, orange rind and mixed spice, and bring the mixture to the boil. Reduce the heat and simmer gently until pulpy — about 15 minutes. Leave to cool. Meanwhile, preheat the oven to 200°C (400°F or Mark 6).

Keep the sheets of phyllo covered with a clean, damp cloth while you work, to prevent them from drying out. Remove one sheet, lay it on a work surface and brush it with melted butter. Cover it with a second sheet of phyllo, brush on more melted butter, then lay a third sheet on top. Cut the layered sheets of phyllo lengthwise into two equal strips, then cut each strip widthwise into four, to give a total of eight 15 by 11 cm (6 by 4½ inch) rectangles.

Divide half of the poppy seed mixture among the eight rectangles: spoon it along one long edge, leaving a 2.5 cm (1 inch) margin free of filling along the edge and at each end. Fold the long edge over just to enclose the filling, fold in the two shorter, side edges, pressing them down gently, then continue rolling up the pastry lengthwise, to make a pillow-shaped parcel. Place the parcel on a baking sheet, seam-side down, and fold the remaining phyllo rectangles in the same way. Use the remaining phyllo sheets and poppy seed mixture to make another eight pillows.

Brush the pillows with a little more melted butter and sprinkle them with the reserved teaspoon of poppy seeds. Bake for 7 to 8 minutes, until crisp and golden. Serve warm or cold.

Tangerine Cream Pastries

Makes 6 pastries
Working time: about 40 minutes
Total time: about 1 hour

Per pastry:			
Calories **105**	4	tangerines	4
Protein **2g**	75 g	granulated sugar	2½ oz
Cholesterol **20mg**	2	sheets phyllo pastry, each about 45 by 30 cm (18 by 12 inches)	2
Total fat **4g**			
Saturated fat **1g**	1 tbsp	safflower oil	1 tbsp
Sodium **15mg**	8 cl	orange-flavoured pastry cream (recipe, page 11)	3 fl oz

Preheat the oven to 220°C (425°F or Mark 7).

Using a potato peeler, thinly pare the rind of two of the tangerines, taking care not to include any pith. Cut the rind into fine shreds. Put the sugar in a saucepan with 12.5 cl (4 fl oz) of water and heat gently, stirring, until the sugar dissolves, then bring it to the boil without stirring. Add the strips of rind to the syrup and simmer them gently for about 20 minutes. Remove the strips with a slotted spoon and leave them to drain in a sieve set over a bowl.

Meanwhile, lightly oil two baking sheets. Lay the sheets of phyllo on a work surface. Using a 9 cm (3½ inch) plain cutter, cut 12 circles from each sheet. Brush the circles very lightly with oil, then stack them, oiled-side up, in pairs on the baking sheets. Bake them until crisp and golden — 4 to 5 minutes. Carefully transfer the 12 paired circles to a wire rack to cool.

Peel the tangerines — including those without the rind — and carefully remove all the pith. Divide them into segments, removing the pips and as much of the membrane as possible. Take six of the paired pastry circles and arrange five or six tangerine segments on each one. Spoon 1 tablespoon of pastry cream over the fruit, then place the remaining pairs of pastry circles on top. Decorate the pastries with the candied orange rind and serve immediately.

Cherry Cheese Tartlets

Makes 12 tartlets
Working time: about 45 minutes
Total time: about 1 hour and 10 minutes

Per tartlet:
Calories **100**
Protein **5g**
Cholesterol **20mg**
Total fat **3g**
Saturated fat **1g**
Sodium **110mg**

3	sheets phyllo pastry, each about 45 by 30 cm (18 by 12 inches)	3
15 g	unsalted butter, melted	½ oz
Spicy cheese filling		
250 g	low-fat soft cheese	8 oz
15 cl	plain low-fat yogurt	¼ pint
1	egg	1
1 tbsp	clear honey	1 tbsp
1 tsp	pure vanilla extract	1 tsp
½ tsp	ground cinnamon	½ tsp
Glossy cherry topping		
1 tbsp	cherry jam	1 tbsp
½ tsp	cornflour	½ tsp
350 g	cherries, stoned and halved	12 oz

Preheat the oven to 190°C (375°F or Mark 5).

Trim 5 cm (2 inches) off one of the short edges of each sheet of phyllo, then cut each sheet into twelve 10 cm (4 inch) squares. Keep the squares covered by a clean, damp cloth to prevent them from drying out, removing them as needed. Brush twelve 7.5 cm (3 inch) individual round tins with a little melted butter. Stack three squares of phyllo pastry in each tin, fold the edges over to neaten them, then brush the tops lightly with melted butter. Bake the cases in the oven until crisp and lightly browned — about 3 minutes. Leave them to cool in the tins.

Meanwhile, prepare the cheese filling. Put the cheese, yogurt, egg, honey, vanilla extract and cinnamon into a mixing bowl. Beat the ingredients together with a wooden spoon until smooth, or blend the mixture in a food processor. Divide the filling among the pastry cases, spreading it evenly with the back of a teaspoon. Return the tartlets to the oven and cook them until the filling has set — 8 to 10 minutes. Remove from the oven and cool the tartlets in the tins while you make the cherry topping.

Make a glaze by stirring the cherry jam with 3 tablespoons of water in a small saucepan set over low heat. Blend the cornflour to a smooth paste with 1 tablespoon of water. Add the cornflour paste to the jam solution, bring to the boil and cook, stirring, until the mixture thickens and clears — about 2 minutes. Arrange the cherry halves on top of the cheese mixture and brush with the cherry glaze. Allow to set for a few minutes before unmoulding and serving.

Cherry Triangles

Makes 12 triangles
Working time: about 40 minutes
Total time: about 1 hour and 20 minutes

Per triangle:			
Calories **90**	125 g	fromage frais	4 oz
Protein **2g**	15 g	caster sugar	½ oz
Cholesterol **0mg**	1 tbsp	kirsch	1 tbsp
Total fat **6g**	500 g	cherries, stoned	1 lb
Saturated fat **trace**	8	sheets phyllo pastry, each about 45 by 30 cm (18 by 12 inches)	8
Sodium **25mg**	3 tsp	safflower oil	3 tsp
		icing sugar, to decorate	

Preheat the oven to 200°C (400°F or Mark 6).

To make the filling, place the *fromage frais*, caster sugar and kirsch in a mixing bowl. Reserve 12 cherries for decoration. Quarter the remainder and gently fold them into the *fromage frais* mixture. Keep the sheets of phyllo covered by a clean, damp cloth to prevent them from drying out, removing them as needed.

Lay one sheet of phyllo on a work surface. Brush it lightly with oil and cover it with a second sheet. Cut this double sheet lengthwise into three strips, each 10 cm (4 inches) wide. Place one tablespoon of filling at one end of a strip, then fold a corner of the phyllo over the filling to form a neat triangle. Continue folding over the filled triangle until you reach the end of the strip, keeping the shape as you work. Tuck in the loose end and transfer the triangular parcel — seam down — to a lightly oiled baking sheet. Make up the two remaining strips in the same way, then make another nine triangles with the remaining phyllo and filling.

Brush the phyllo triangles with the remaining oil and bake them until they are crisp and golden — 9 to 10 minutes. Transfer them to a wire rack to cool.

Before serving, halve the remaining cherries. Sift a little icing sugar over the top of each triangle and serve with the cherries.

Fruited Phyllo Cigars

Makes 24 cigars
Working time: about 25 minutes
Total time: about 9 hours and 45 minutes
(includes soaking and cooling)

Per cigar:
Calories **35**
Protein **trace**
Cholesterol **0mg**
Total fat **2g**
Saturated fat **0g**
Sodium **15mg**

175 g	mixed dried fruits (peaches, pears apple rings, apricots), finely chopped	6 oz
2 tsp	ground coriander	2 tsp
1½ tbsp	safflower oil	1½ tbsp
2	sheets phyllo pastry, each about 45 by 30 cm (18 by 12 inches)	2
2 tbsp	icing sugar	2 tbsp

Put the mixed dried fruits into a small, non-reactive saucepan, pour over about 17.5 cl (6 fl oz) of boiling water, cover the pan and leave the fruit to soak for 8 hours, or overnight.

When the fruit is plump, place the pan over a low heat and simmer the fruit, uncovered, until it is soft and the water has evaporated. Remove the pan from the heat, stir in the coriander and leave the fruit to cool.

Preheat the oven to 180°C (350°F or Mark 4).

Lightly oil a large baking sheet. Lay one sheet of phyllo on top of the other. Cut the sheets lengthwise into four equal strips, then cut each strip widthwise into three, to give a total of twenty-four 15 by 7.5 cm (6 by 3 inch) rectangles. Stack them together in one pile. Brush the top rectangle with a little oil and place a teaspoonful of the cooled fruit mixture along one of its shorter edges, leaving a 1 cm (½ inch) margin at either end of the filling. Roll up the phyllo round the fruit to form a ''cigar'', then place the cigar, seam underneath, on the baking sheet. Brush the next rectangle with oil and repeat the process, continuing until all the filling and phyllo have been used.

Bake the cigars for 15 to 20 minutes, until they are crisp and golden. Transfer them to a wire rack to cool, and sift the icing sugar over them before serving.

Chocolate Fruit Phyllo Flowers

Makes 4 flowers
Working time: about 35 minutes
Total time: about 50 minutes

Per flower:			
Calories **155**	4	sheets phyllo pastry, each about 45 by 30 cm (18 by 12 inches)	4
Protein **4g**			
Cholesterol **10mg**	15 g	unsalted butter, melted	½ oz
Total fat **9g**	45 g	plain chocolate	1 ½ oz
Saturated fat **4g**	125 g	fromage frais	4 oz
Sodium **35mg**	4	strawberries, hulled and sliced	4
	10	green grapes, halved and seeded	10

Preheat the oven to 190°C (375°F or Mark 5).

Cut each sheet of phyllo in half lengthwise, then in four widthwise, to give a total of thirty-two 15 by 11 cm (6 by 4½ inch) rectangles of pastry. Keep the rec-tangles covered with a clean, damp cloth to prevent them from drying out, removing them as required.

Brush four 10 cm (4 inch) shallow tartlet tins with a little melted butter. Line one tin with four pieces of phyllo arranged at different angles, brush lightly with melted butter, then arrange another four layers of phyllo on top at different angles from the first batch. Line each tin with pastry in the same way, then lightly brush the top layer with melted butter.

Bake the phyllo in the oven for 6 to 8 minutes, until crisp and golden-brown, then allow to cool in the tins.

Melt the chocolate in a heatproof bowl set over a pan of hot, but not boiling, water. Using a fine brush, paint the inside of the phyllo cases with half of the melted chocolate.

Place the *fromage frais* in a bowl and blend in the remaining chocolate. Divide the *fromage frais* mixture among the phyllo flower cases, and arrange the straw-berry slices and grape halves to resemble petals. Carefully unmould the flowers and serve immediately.

Kataifi Nests with Orange-Flower Custard

KATAIFI IS A GREEK PASTRY MADE IN LONG, THIN STRANDS LIKE VERMICELLI. IT CAN BE BOUGHT READY-MADE FROM MIDDLE EASTERN SPECIALITY SHOPS; IF UNAVAILABLE, PHYLLO CAN BE SUBSTITUTED, CUT AND SHAPED AS IN ALMOND AND PERSIMMON STARS ON PAGE 62.

Makes 16 nests
Working time: about 1 hour
Total time: about 2 hours (includes soaking)

Per nest:
Calories **70**
Protein **3g**
Cholesterol **20mg**
Total fat **2g**
Saturated fat **1g**
Sodium **15mg**

250 g	kataifi pastry, at room temperature	8 oz
20 g	unsalted butter, melted	¾ oz
75 g	dried apricots, 60 g (2 oz) soaked in water for 30 minutes, soaking water reserved, remainder diced	2½ oz
1	stick cinnamon	1
2.5 cm	strip lemon rind	1 inch
2 tbsp	fresh lemon juice	2 tbsp
1 tbsp	clear honey	1 tbsp
60 g	thick Greek yogurt	2 oz
½ tsp	ground cinnamon	½ tsp
Orange-flower custard		
2 tsp	cornflour	2 tsp
15 cl	skimmed milk	¼ pint
1	egg yolk	1
2 tsp	clear honey	2 tsp
1 tsp	pure vanilla extract	1 tsp
1 tsp	orange-flower water	1 tsp
½ tsp	finely-grated orange rind	½ tsp
1 tbsp	powdered gelatine	1 tbsp

Preheat the oven to 190°C (375°F or Mark 5).

Knead the kataifi pastry, while still in the packet, to soften the strands and ease separation. Remove the required quantity from the packet and tease out the strands a little more with your hands. Divide the kataifi into 16 equal portions. Press one portion into a 5 cm (2 inch) bun tin, forming a small nest of pastry by pressing down in the centre and up the sides of the tin. Brush the nest with a little of the melted butter. Form the other 15 nests in the same way, then bake them until they are golden-brown — about 20 minutes. Turn them out to cool on a wire rack.

While the nests are baking, put the soaked apricots and their soaking water into a saucepan and add the cinnamon stick, lemon rind, lemon juice and honey. Bring the liquid to the boil, then reduce the heat and simmer until the apricots are tender — about 20 minutes; top up the water as necessary. Using a slotted spoon, transfer the apricots to a plate and let them cool. Strain the liquid, then return it to the pan and boil it down until only 4 tablespoons remain; reserve this syrup for glazing the pastries.

To make the custard, mix the cornflour to a smooth paste with 1 tablespoon of the skimmed milk. Beat the egg yolk with the honey, then blend in the cornflour. Heat the remaining milk in a pan until it is near boiling point, then whisk it into the egg mixture. Return the custard to the pan and simmer it gently until it has thickened, stirring all the time. Strain the custard through a fine sieve, then beat in the vanilla extract, orange-flower water and orange rind. Sprinkle the gelatine over 2 tablespoons of water in a small bowl and allow it to stand for 2 minutes. Place the bowl over a pan of simmering water and stir until the gelatine has dissolved. Add the gelatine to the custard, whisking vigorously. Set it aside to cool, covering the surface closely with plastic film to prevent a skin forming.

Finely dice the cooked apricots. Whisk the cooled custard, then fold in the cooked apricots and the yogurt. Spoon a little of this filling into the hollow of each kataifi nest. Using a pastry brush, sprinkle a little of the reserved syrup round the edges of each nest, and decorate the filling with a piece of diced dried apricot and a sprinkling of ground cinnamon. Serve at room temperature or chilled.

Pumpkin and Pistachio Pastries

Makes 6 pastries
Working time: about 45 minutes
Total time: about 1 hour and 45 minutes

Per pastry:
Calories **175**
Protein **4g**
Cholesterol **20mg**
Total fat **10g**
Saturated fat **3g**
Sodium **135mg**

500 g	slice of pumpkin	1 lb
45 g	shelled pistachio nuts	1 ½ oz
1 tbsp	clear honey	1 tbsp
2 tbsp	ginger syrup, from stem ginger jar	2 tbsp
2 tbsp	fresh lemon juice	2 tbsp
1 tsp	ground cinnamon	1 tsp
½ tsp	grated nutmeg	½ tsp
200 g	thick Greek yogurt	7 oz
1	egg white	1
¼ tsp	salt	¼ tsp
6	sheets phyllo pastry, each about 45 by 30 cm (18 by 12 inches)	6
30 g	unsalted butter, melted	1 oz
1 tbsp	light brown sugar	1 tbsp
2 tsp	icing sugar	2 tsp

Place the pumpkin slice, skin side down, in a steamer set over a saucepan of lightly boiling water and steam until tender — 20 to 30 minutes. Meanwhile, blanch the pistachio nuts in boiling water for 1 minute, drain them thoroughly, then rub them vigorously in a towel to remove their skins. Roughly chop the nuts.

Peel the pumpkin slice, chop the flesh roughly and purée it in a blender with the honey, ginger syrup, lemon juice, cinnamon and nutmeg. Transfer the purée to a mixing bowl. Reserve 1 tablespoon of yogurt for decoration, and stir the remainder into the purée, mixing well. In a separate bowl, whisk the egg white with the salt until it forms soft peaks. Fold it gently but thoroughly into the pumpkin purée and put the mixture in the refrigerator to chill.

Preheat the oven to 180°C (350°F or Mark 4).

Lay one sheet of phyllo pastry on a work surface, keeping the others covered by a clean, damp cloth to prevent them from drying out. Fold the sheet in half widthwise, to make a 30 by 22.5 cm (12 by 9 inch) rectangle. Brush it lightly with a little of the melted butter. Sprinkle one sixth of the pistachio nuts along one long edge of the pastry rectangle, leaving 2.5 cm (1 inch) free of nuts at each end. Sprinkle the nuts with a little of the brown sugar.

Fold the long edge of pastry over to enclose the nuts, then fold in 1 cm (½ inch) of pastry along the length of each short side, and press down to seal. Roll up the nut filling until only a 4 cm (1½ inch) strip of phyllo remains unrolled. Shape the pastry into a ring, with the unrolled strip of phyllo inside, so that the nut-filled roll forms a rim. Overlap the ends of the rim, brush the inside facing edges with melted butter and press them together to ensure a good seal. To form the base of the case, lift the pastry off the work surface and neatly pleat and flatten the unrolled phyllo towards the centre. Brush the folds with butter, place the case on a flat surface again, and press all the folds and seals firmly together. Repeat this process with the other five phyllo sheets.

Place the pastry cases on a lightly-greased baking sheet and bake them until they are crisp and deep golden-brown — about 20 minutes. Turn them out carefully on to a wire rack to cool.

Shortly before serving, sift a little icing sugar over each pastry rim, and spoon the pumpkin purée into the pastry cases. Beat the reserved yogurt until it is smooth and swirl a little in the centre of each pastry.

EDITOR'S NOTE: *Clear honey may be substituted for the stem ginger syrup.*

Almond and Persimmon Stars

Makes 12 stars
Working time: about 30 minutes
Total time: about 1 hour and 10 minutes

Per star:
Calories **60**
Protein **1g**
Cholesterol **0mg**
Total fat **5g**
Saturated fat **1g**
Sodium **35mg**

1	sheet phyllo pastry, about 45 by 30 cm (18 by 12 inches)	1
30 g	polyunsaturated margarine, melted	1 oz
2	persimmons, peeled, one chopped, one sliced	2
3 tbsp	ground almonds	3 tbsp
2 tbsp	ground amaretti biscuits	2 tbsp
1	egg white	1

Grease and lightly flour twelve 7.5 cm (3 inch) shallow, flat-based tartlet tins. Preheat the oven to 200°C (400°F or Mark 6).

Spread the phyllo out on a work surface and brush it with the melted margarine. Cut the sheet into twenty-four 7.5 cm (3 inch) squares. Line each tartlet tin with two squares of phyllo, arranging the corners to form an eight-pointed star.

To make the filling, purée the chopped persimmon in a blender or food processor. Transfer the purée to a mixing bowl and stir in the ground almonds and amaretti biscuit crumbs. In a separate bowl, whisk the egg white until it is stiff, then fold it gently into the persimmon-amaretti mixture.

Distribute the filling among the phyllo stars and bake them until the pastry is golden — 15 to 20 minutes. Allow the stars to cool briefly in their tins, then un-mould them on to wire racks to cool completely.

Decorate each star with the slices of persimmon. Serve the stars on the day they are baked, while the pastry is still crisp.

EDITOR'S NOTE: *If amaretti biscuits are unobtainable, crumbled almond macaroons, or any other crumbled sweet biscuits, may be substituted.*

Phyllo Fruit Squares

Makes 10 squares
Working time: about 30 minutes
Total time: about 1 hour and 25 minutes

Per square:
Calories **135**
Protein **6g**
Cholesterol **trace**
Total fat **3g**
Saturated fat **2g**
Sodium **25mg**

30 g	unsalted butter, melted	1 oz
1	large orange, rind grated, peel and pith removed, flesh cut into segments (page 41)	1
90 g	raisins	3 oz
90 g	sultanas	3 oz
1	large cooking apple, peeled and grated	1
10	sheets phyllo pastry, each about 45 by 30 cm (18 by 12 inches)	10
3 tsp	clear honey	3 tsp
1 tbsp	flaked almonds	1 tbsp
1 tbsp	caster sugar	1 tbsp
2 tsp	orange-flower water	2 tsp

Preheat the oven to 190°C (375°F or Mark 5). Brush a 28 by 18 by 4 cm (11 by 7 by 1½ inch) baking tin with a little of the melted butter.

Chop the orange segments and add them to the bowl with the raisins, sultanas, apple and 2 teaspoons of the orange rind. Mix the fruit well together.

Keep the sheets of phyllo covered by a clean, damp cloth to prevent them drying out, removing them as required. Lay one sheet of phyllo pastry in the prepared tin so that it overhangs all four sides of the tin. Brush it sparingly with melted butter and cover it with another sheet of phyllo. Brush this with butter and cover it with a third sheet. Sprinkle one third of the fruit mixture over the phyllo in the tin and dribble 1 teaspoon of the honey over the fruit. Fold the four overhanging edges over the filling, one after another, and brush these folded edges with butter.

Repeat the above procedure to make two more layers of phyllo and filling. Lay the final sheet of phyllo over the top, neatly folding the four edges underneath. Brush the top with butter and lightly mark it into a lattice design with a knife. Sprinkle over the almonds.

Bake in the oven until golden-brown — 25 to 30 minutes. Towards the end of the baking time, prepare a syrup. Heat the sugar and orange-flower water in a small saucepan with 2 tablespoons of water. Stir the mixture gently until the sugar has dissolved, then boil it for 1 minute.

Remove the baked phyllo fruit pastry from the oven and pour the syrup over the top. Allow to cool before cutting into squares and serving.

2 *Hazelnut meringue piped into rows of shells awaits the long, gentle cooking that will dry and crisp it (recipe, page 87).*

Light and Airy Creations

Feathery sponges, ethereal meringues and yeast-leavened cakes all have one essential ingredient in common: air. It is air that gives these items of patisserie their lightness and sublime texture.

Genoese sponge, containing the minimum amount of butter *(page 11)*, is the foundation for many of the assemblies on pages 66 to 80. Air trapped within eggs as they are whisked with sugar expands and raises the flour and butter mixture during baking. To retain as much air as possible when adding the flour and butter, fold them gently into the eggs with a large metal spoon or spatula, rather than stirring them in. The melted butter must be as cool as possible, or its warmth will tend to break down air bubbles. Bake the sponge immediately, since it will deflate if left to stand. Any trimmings need not be wasted; use them to make such delicacies as apricot and hazelnut petits fours *(page 113)* or chocolate-dipped stuffed prunes *(page 126)*.

Meringues are nothing more than a magical blend of egg whites, sugar and air. When beaten vigorously, the egg whites trap air in myriad bubbles. The addition of sugar reinforces the structure of the mixture and makes it firm enough to pipe out. Before the sugar is added, the whites should be whisked until they hold a peak. Add the sugar in small batches, whisking well between each addition to return the mixture to a stiff peak. Egg whites and sugar whisked over hot water produce a denser-textured meringue particularly suitable for piping into nests and other containers, as in the fruit-filled meringue baskets on page 91.

Whatever the method of preparation, meringues require long, slow cooking in the oven to preserve their snow-white colour and produce the desired crispness. Some ovens can be a little too hot even at the recommended setting. If in doubt, set your oven to the lowest heat and adjust the cooking time, if necessary. The meringues are ready when they can be lifted easily from the baking paper.

Yeast cakes, rich in B vitamins, are naturally self-raising. Yeast is a living organism that gives off carbon dioxide when it is mixed with a liquid, flour and sugar. Trapped within the gluten structure of the dough by kneading, the gas gradually expands the mixture, increasing its volume threefold. Warmth accelerates the process, but the yeast will be killed if overheated; normal warm kitchen temperatures are ideal. When a firmer dough is required, as it is for the brioche peaches on page 94 and the Danish pastries on page 98, it must be allowed to rise slowly by being placed in a refrigerator for up to 5 hours.

Pineapple Sponge Sandwiches

Makes 12 sandwiches
Working time: about 55 minutes
Total time: about 1 hour and 30 minutes

Per sandwich:
Calories **60**
Protein **1g**
Cholesterol **25mg**
Total fat **2g**
Saturated fat **1g**
Sodium **10mg**

300 g	finely chopped fresh pineapple	10 oz
	icing sugar, to decorate	
Genoese sponge		
2	cardamom pods, seeds only	2
1	egg	1
1	egg white	1
45 g	caster sugar	1 ½ oz
60 g	plain flour	2 oz
15 g	unsalted butter, melted and cooled	½ oz

Preheat the oven to 180°C (350°F or Mark 4). Line two large baking sheets with non-stick parchment paper.

To make the sponge, first toast the cardamom seeds in a dry, heavy-bottomed non-stick pan, then crush them very finely. Following the method on page 11, prepare the genoese sponge with the ingredients listed above, adding the crushed cardamom seeds to the flour. Using a rubber spatula, spread out the batter in twelve 6 cm (2½ inch) circles on the baking sheets, making sure that the edges are no thinner than the centres. Bake for about 6 minutes, or until very lightly coloured and set — the edges should not become brown. Immediately the circles are removed from the oven, carefully transfer them to a wire rack to cool.

Divide the chopped pineapple into 12 equal portions. Just before serving, place a portion of pineapple on half of each sponge circle and carefully fold over the other half. Sift icing sugar over the top. Heat a long, metal skewer over a flame or an electric ring, protecting your hand with an oven glove. When the skewer is red hot, brand a crisscross pattern on the sponges by laying the skewer briefly on the icing sugar, reheating the skewer if necessary.

Layered Fruit Sponges

Makes 8 sponges
Working time: about 1 hour
Total time: about 1 hour and 10 minutes

Per sponge:
Calories **200**
Protein **7g**
Cholesterol **115mg**
Total fat **6g**
Saturated fat **2g**
Sodium **35mg**

2	eggs	2
1	egg white	1
90 g	caster sugar	3 oz
90 g	plain flour	3 oz
1 tbsp	cocoa powder	1 tbsp
1 tbsp	icing sugar	1 tbsp
Fruit and almond filling		
250 g	cherries, eight reserved whole for decoration, remainder stoned and chopped	8 oz
2	nectarines, blanched in boiling water for 30 seconds, skinned, stoned and chopped	2
30 cl	pastry cream (recipe, page 11), made with ½ tsp pure almond extract instead of 1 tsp vanilla	½ pint

Preheat the oven to 180°C (350°F or Mark 4). Line three baking sheets with non-stick parchment paper. Draw eight 7.5 cm (3 inch) circles in pencil, spaced evenly apart, on each paper sheet; invert the paper so the marks face downwards.

Put the eggs, egg white and caster sugar into a mixing bowl. Place the bowl over a saucepan of hot, but not boiling, water over low heat. Whisk the eggs and sugar together with an electric hand-held mixer until thick and very pale. Remove the bowl from the saucepan and continue whisking until the mixture is cool and falls from the whisk in a ribbon trail. Pour half of the mixture into another bowl. Sift half of the flour plus 1 tablespoon over the surface of the mixture in one bowl, then fold it in very gently using a large metal spoon. Fold the remaining flour and the cocoa powder into the mixture in the other bowl.

Transfer the mixtures into separate nylon piping bags, each fitted with a 5 mm (¼ inch) plain nozzle. Pipe 12 rings with the cocoa-flavoured mixture, following the outlines drawn on the parchment paper,

and pipe a chocolate dot in the centre of each. Fill in the centre rings with plain mixture. Outline the remaining 12 circles with plain mixture, pipe a plain dot in the centre, and fill the centre rings with chocolate mixture.

Bake until the sponge rounds feel firm and are lightly browned — about 5 minutes. Cool on the paper for 2 minutes, then with a metal spatula remove them to a wire rack and leave to cool fully.

Mix together the chopped cherries and nectarines for the filling, then assemble the sponges. Spread a little pastry cream over a sponge round and sprinkle it with chopped mixed fruit. Place another sponge on top, cover it with pastry cream and fruit, and top with a third sponge round. Make up seven more layered sponges in the same way.

Sift a little icing sugar over the tops of the sponges and place a whole cherry in the centre. Serve within an hour of assembling.

Cornets Filled with Fruit Cream

Makes 30 cornets
Working time: about 50 minutes
Total time: about 1 hour and 20 minutes

Per cornet:
Calories **50**
Protein **1g**
Cholesterol **15mg**
Total fat **2g**
Saturated fat **1g**
Sodium **15mg**

2	egg whites	2
60 g	caster sugar	2 oz
60 g	plain flour	2 oz
60 g	unsalted butter, melted and cooled	2 oz
60 g	mixed candied peel, finely chopped	2 oz
30 cl	pastry cream (recipe, page 11)	½ pint

Preheat the oven to 190°C (375°F or Mark 5). Line two large baking sheets with non-stick parchment paper.

To make the cornets, first whisk the egg whites in a mixing bowl until they are frothy. Sprinkle the sugar over the surface and whisk for 2 to 3 minutes, until thick and shiny. Sift the flour over the surface, then fold it in very gently with the melted butter. Drop 2 to 3 teaspoonfuls of mixture, spaced well apart, on to one of the baking sheets. Spread each spoonful out with the back of a spoon to form a circle 6 to 7.5 cm (2½ to 3 inches) in diameter. Bake for about 5 minutes, or until the edges are a light golden-brown. Meanwhile, make two or three more circles on the second sheet.

Remove the baked circles from the oven, and insert the second baking sheet. Quickly but carefully remove each of the baked circles in turn with a metal spatula, and mould it round a metal cream horn mould until set in shape. If the circles start to harden before they are all shaped, return them to the oven for a minute or so to soften them. Transfer the cornets to a wire rack to cool completely. Bake and shape the remaining mixture in the same way.

Just before serving, fold three quarters of the mixed candied peel into the pastry cream and spoon it into the sponge cornets. Decorate the filling with the remaining peel and serve.

Filigree Lime Baskets

Makes 8 baskets
Working time: about 40 minutes
Total time: about 1 hour

Per basket:		
Calories **170**	2	egg whites	2
Protein **3g**	45 g	icing sugar, sifted	1 ½ oz
Cholesterol **65mg**	30 g	ground rice	1 oz
Total fat **5g**	30 g	cornflour	1 oz
Saturated fat **2g**	30 g	plain flour, sifted	1 oz
Sodium **35mg**	30 g	unsalted butter, melted	1 oz
	½ tsp	pure vanilla extract	½ tsp
	Whipped lime filling		
	2	limes	2
	2	egg yolks	2
	90 g	caster sugar	3 oz
	2 tsp	powdered gelatine	2 tsp
	3	egg whites	3
	2 tbsp	fromage frais	2 tbsp
	125 g	strawberries, hulled and sliced	4 oz

Preheat the oven to 220°C (425°F or Mark 7). Line a baking sheet with non-stick parchment paper. Draw four 10 cm (4 inch) circles on the paper, then invert it so that the markings face downwards.

Whisk the egg whites in a clean, grease-free bowl until they are white and frothy. Add the icing sugar and whisk until it is well blended, then whisk in the ground rice, cornflour and flour. Pour in the melted butter and vanilla and whisk until all the ingredients are thoroughly blended. Leave the mixture to thicken for a few minutes, then transfer it to a piping bag *(page 13)* made with two thicknesses of greaseproof paper.

Snip the pointed end off the bag to make a 3 mm (⅛ inch) opening. Pipe a series of parallel lines, spaced 1 cm (½ inch) apart, within one of the marked circles; then pipe a second series of lines, at right angles to the first, to form a lattice. Finally, pipe a scalloped edge round the outside of the circle, to join up the ends of the piped lines. Pipe another three lattice rounds in the same way.

Bake the lattice rounds until they are set and pale — about 2 minutes. Loosen them with a metal spatula and return them to the oven until they are pale gold around the edges — 1 to 2 minutes.

Have ready a small, warm bowl for shaping the rounds into baskets. Lift the rounds, one at a time, and lightly press them into the bowl. If the rounds begin to set before they have been shaped, return them to the oven for a few seconds. Cool the baskets on a wire rack. Make another four baskets with the remaining mixture, using the same parchment paper but placing it on a second, cool, baking sheet.

To prepare the filling, cut three 1 cm (½ inch) wide strips of rind from one of the limes and slice them into needle-thin shreds. Boil them in a little water until they are tender — about 3 minutes. Drain the shreds and set them aside.

Grate the remaining rind from the limes and squeeze the juice. Whisk together the egg yolks and caster sugar until thick, then stir in the lime juice and grated rind. Sprinkle the gelatine over 2 tablespoons of water in a small bowl and leave it to soften for 2 minutes. Place the bowl over a saucepan of simmering water and stir until the gelatine has dissolved. Beat the gelatine solution into the lime and egg yolks, and let the mixture stand until it begins to set — about 15 minutes at room temperature.

Whisk the egg whites until stiff but not dry. Whisk the *fromage frais* into the partly set egg and lime mixture, then fold in the whites until the mixture is evenly blended. Leave until just set — 15 to 20 minutes.

Place the filigree baskets on individual serving plates and spoon in the lime filling. Decorate with the strawberry slices and the reserved shreds of lime.

Oatmeal Blueberry Galettes

Makes 10 galettes
Working time: about 1 hour
Total time: about 1 hour and 30 minutes

Per galette:
Calories **115**
Protein **3g**
Cholesterol **10mg**
Total fat **5g**
Saturated fat **3g**
Sodium **20mg**

2	egg whites	2
60 g	icing sugar, sifted	2 oz
30 g	medium oatmeal	1 oz
30 g	plain flour, sifted	1 oz
30 g	unsalted butter, melted	1 oz
30	fresh blueberries, picked over and stemmed, to decorate	30
30	small petal shapes cut from thin strips of orange rind, to decorate	30
Creamy blueberry filling		
200 g	fromage frais	7 oz
1 tbsp	icing sugar, sifted	1 tbsp
1 tsp	finely grated orange rind	1 tsp
300 g	fresh blueberries, picked over and stemmed	10 oz

Preheat the oven to 200°C (400°F or Mark 6). Line two baking sheets with non-stick parchment paper. Draw six 7.5 cm (3 inch) circles in pencil, spaced well apart, on each sheet of paper and invert them so that the marks face downwards.

Whisk the egg whites in a clean, grease-free bowl until they are white and frothy. Add 45 g (1½ oz) of the icing sugar and whisk until it is dissolved, then whisk in the oatmeal and flour. Finally, pour in the butter and whisk thoroughly. Place a teaspoonful of the mixture in the middle of each circle; using a small metal spatula, spread the mixture within the circles.

Bake the rounds until they are golden at the edges — 3 to 4 minutes. Let them rest on the parchment paper for 30 seconds, then lift them off with a metal spatula and cool them on a wire rack. Repeat the procedure, re-using the parchment paper for each batch, until the mixture is used up. There should be a total of 30 rounds.

For the filling, mix together the *fromage frais*, sugar and orange rind, then gently stir in the blueberries.

Assemble the galettes about 30 minutes before serving. Place one round on a work surface, spread it with a little filling and cover with another round, spread this with more filling and top the assembly with a third round. Make up the rest of the rounds and filling into galettes in the same way. Sift a little icing sugar over the tops of the galettes and decorate each one with three blueberries and three orange rind petals.

EDITOR'S NOTE: *Any soft fruit in season, or a mixture of summer berries, can replace the blueberries.*

Preheat the oven to 190°C (375°F or Mark 5). Butter twelve 7.5 cm (3 inch) dimple moulds, dust them lightly with flour and place them on baking sheets.

Following the method on page 11, prepare a genoese sponge mixture using the ingredients listed here. Fill each dimple mould almost to the top with sponge mixture and bake them until the sponge is well risen, lightly browned and springy to the touch — 10 to 15 minutes. Carefully unmould the ring cakes on to a wire rack to cool.

Put the 30 g (1 oz) of caster sugar and 2 table-spoons of kirsch in a small non-reactive saucepan with 2 tablespoons of cold water and heat gently. When the sugar has dissolved, boil the syrup rapidly for 1 minute, then remove it from the heat.

Cut each ring cake in half horizontally, keeping matching pairs together, cut sides uppermost. Brush each cut surface with a little of the kirsch syrup.

To make the filling, whisk together the egg white, sugar, kirsch and cream until the mixture will hold a peak. Spoon the filling into a piping bag fitted with a 5 mm (¼ inch) star nozzle. Pipe the cream decoratively over the bottom half of each cake, and replace the tops. Sift the icing sugar over the cakes, then pipe a whirl of cream into their centres. Decorate with the sugar-frosted rose and freesia petals.

Petal Ring Cakes

Makes 12 cakes
Working time: about 50 minutes
Total time: about 1 hour and 25 minutes

Per cake:
Calories **140**
Protein **2g**
Cholesterol **60mg**
Total fat **8g**
Saturated fat **4g**
Sodium **25mg**

30 g	caster sugar	1 oz
2 tbsp	kirsch	2 tbsp
1 tbsp	icing sugar	1 tbsp
12	sugar-frosted rose petals (box, right)	12
12	sugar-frosted freesia petals (box, right)	12
	Genoese sponge	
2	eggs	2
1	egg white	1
60 g	caster sugar	2 oz
90 g	plain flour	3 oz
15 g	unsalted butter, melted and cooled	½ oz
	Kirsch cream filling	
1	egg white	1
1 tsp	caster sugar	1 tsp
1 tsp	kirsch	1 tsp
15 cl	double cream	¼ pint

Sugar-Frosted Petals

APPLYING A COATING. Beat an egg white until it lightens without foaming. Brush violet, primrose, freesia or — as here — rose petals with the white, then dip them in caster sugar. Transfer them to a plate and leave in a warm place until dry and hard. In an airtight container, they will keep for weeks.

Harlequins

Makes 24 harlequins
Working time: about 1 hour and 10 minutes
Total time: about 2 hours (includes chilling)

Per harlequin:
Calories **60**
Protein **1g**
Cholesterol **20mg**
Total fat **2g**
Saturated fat **1g**
Sodium **10mg**

3	peaches, halved and stoned	3
250 g	fresh raspberries	8 oz
250 g	fresh blackcurrants, topped and tailed	8 oz
3 tbsp	caster sugar	3 tbsp
2 tbsp	powdered gelatine	2 tbsp
6 tbsp	fromage frais	6 tbsp
	peach slices, raspberries and blackcurrants, to decorate	
	Genoese sponge	
2	eggs	2
1	egg white	1
90 g	caster sugar	3 oz
90 g	plain flour	3 oz
15 g	unsalted butter, melted and cooled	½ oz

Following the method on page 11, prepare a genoese sponge with the ingredients listed above; bake for 10 to 15 minutes only, then unmould and cool.

Put the peaches, raspberries and blackcurrants into three separate non-reactive saucepans, each with 2 tablespoons of water and 1 tablespoon of the caster sugar. Cook them gently, shaking the pans occa-sionally, until the fruits are tender — 3 to 4 minutes. Purée the three fruits separately in a food processor or blender. Sieve each purée and keep them separate.

Sprinkle the gelatine over 6 tablespoons of water in a bowl and leave it to soften for 2 minutes. Place the bowl over a saucepan of simmering water and stir until the gelatine has completely dissolved. Stir one third of the gelatine solution into each fruit purée, then whisk 2 tablespoons of the *fromage frais* into each. Chill the fruit mixtures in the refrigerator until they are just be-ginning to set — 10 to 15 minutes.

Meanwhile, take the baking tin in which the sponge was cooked and line the base with a piece of foil long enough to stand 4 cm (1½ inches) above the rim of the tin on the two short sides; this will ease removal of the finished assembly later. Replace the sponge.

Spread the blackcurrant mixture evenly over the sponge, then chill it for 5 minutes to firm it up. Spread a peach layer over the blackcurrant and chill again, then repeat with the raspberry mixture. Chill for at least 30 minutes, until the fruit layers have set firmly.

Holding the aluminium foil "handles", lift the sponge out of the tin. Carefully peel back the foil and trim the edges of the assembly, then cut it into diamonds, triangles or squares and arrange on a serving plate. Decorate the top of each harlequin with pieces of fruit.

Blackcurrant Charlottes

Makes 12 charlottes
Working time: about 1 hour
Total time: about 3 hours and 15 minutes

Per charlotte:
Calories **220**
Protein **5g**
Cholesterol **60mg**
Total fat **6g**
Saturated fat **3g**
Sodium **20mg**

250 g	fresh blackcurrants, picked over, or frozen blackcurrants, thawed	8 oz
4 tbsp	crème de cassis	4 tbsp
250 g	fromage frais	8 oz
30 g	caster sugar	1 oz
2½ tsp	powdered gelatine	2½ tsp
1	genoese sponge (recipe, page 11)	1
125 g	icing sugar	4 oz

First, make a mousse for the filling. Purée the blackcurrants in a food processor or blender. Then add the *crème de cassis*, *fromage frais* and caster sugar, and process for about 30 seconds, until smoothly blended. Sprinkle the gelatine over 2 tablespoons of water in a small bowl. Leave it to soften for 2 minutes, then place the bowl over a pan of simmering water and stir until the gelatine has completely dissolved. Add the gelatine solution to the blackcurrant mixture and process for a further 20 seconds. Set the mousse aside.

Line the bases of twelve 7.5 cl (2½ fl oz) dariole moulds with a circle of parchment paper. Oil the sides of the moulds with a little almond oil or other flavourless oil.

Trim off the outer crusts from the rectangle of genoese sponge and, with a long, sharp knife, cut the sponge in half horizontally. Using the top of a dariole mould, stamp out 12 sponge circles from one of the sheets, then cut 12 small rounds that will fit into the bottom of the moulds. Cut the remaining sponge into thin finger slices, about 2.5 cm (1 inch) wide and long enough to line the moulds from base to top.

Place the small sponge rounds in the bottoms of the moulds. Using a rolling pin, flatten each sponge finger, then line the moulds with the fingers, removing any surplus that overhangs the top. Do not worry if there are gaps in the lining of the moulds — the mousse will show through in stripes and look pretty.

Fill each lined mould with mousse until it is level with the top. Lightly place a sponge circle on top of each, then refrigerate the charlottes for at least 1½ hours.

Just before serving, loosen the sides of each charlotte with a thin knife and turn out on to a serving plate. Remove the circle of lining paper.

Prepare a glacé icing by mixing the icing sugar with 4 teaspoons of water until smooth. Apply the icing with a small metal spatula and allow it to drip down the sides of the charlottes.

Pear and Fig Slices

Makes 16 slices
Working time: about 2 hours
Total time: about 6 hours (includes chilling)

Per slice:
Calories **150**
Protein **4g**
Cholesterol **45mg**
Total fat **3g**
Saturated fat **1g**
Sodium **50mg**

1 tsp	fresh lemon juice	1 tsp
30 g	vanilla sugar	1 oz
500 g	firm pears, peeled, cored and cut lengthwise into 1 cm (½ inch) slices	1 lb
1	genoese sponge (recipe, page 11), baked in a 38 by 25 cm (15 by 10 inch) tin for 20 to 25 minutes	1
5	fresh figs, peeled, sliced lengthwise into eighths	5
1 tbsp	icing sugar, sifted	1 tbsp
½ tsp	cocoa powder	½ tsp
Custard mousse		
30 cl	skimmed milk	½ pint
½	vanilla pod, split	½
30 g	cornflour	1 oz
2	egg whites	2
125 g	caster sugar	4 oz
1 tbsp	lemon juice	1 tbsp
2 tbsp	apple juice	2 tbsp
1 tbsp	powdered gelatine	1 tbsp
2 tsp	pure vanilla extract	2 tsp
2 tbsp	Marsala	2 tbsp
90 g	thick Greek yogurt	3 oz

Put the lemon juice and vanilla sugar in a pan with 30 cl (½ pint) of water and bring to the boil. Reduce the heat, add the pear slices, and poach them very gently until they are soft and translucent — 4 to 5 minutes. Carefully remove the pear slices from the liquid, let them cool to room temperature, then chill them in the refrigerator. Strain the poaching syrup through a fine sieve, return it to the pan, and boil it until only 5 tablespoons remain. Set the reduced syrup aside.

To make the custard mousse, put the milk and vanilla pod into a saucepan and heat very gently. Blend the cornflour with 2 tablespoons of the heated milk in a mixing bowl. Bring the rest of the milk to near boiling, then whisk it into the cornflour. Return the mixture to the pan, bring it to the boil, beat it well, and simmer for a further 5 minutes, stirring continuously. Remove the custard from the heat. Strain the mixture through a nylon sieve into a bowl, cover the surface closely with plastic film to prevent a skin forming, and allow it to cool to room temperature.

Meanwhile, put the egg whites and caster sugar in a large bowl set over a saucepan of simmering water; the bowl should not touch the water. Whisk gently until the sugar has melted, then whisk more vigorously until the mixture is thick and glossy and holds a trail across the surface. Remove the bowl from the saucepan and whisk until the meringue cools to room temperature and is very stiff. Set the meringue aside.

Combine the lemon juice and apple juice in a small bowl and sprinkle on the gelatine. Allow the gelatine to soften for 2 minutes, then place the bowl over a saucepan of simmering water and stir until the gelatine has dissolved. Let it cool a little. Stir the vanilla extract and Marsala into the cooled custard, then whisk in the dissolved gelatine. When the mixture is thick and creamy, blend the yogurt into the custard. Stir 1 tablespoon of meringue into the custard until it is well blended, then gently fold in the rest of the meringue. Keep the custard mousse at room temperature while preparing the tin.

Brush almond oil, or another flavourless oil, over the base and sides of a 38 by 7.5 cm (15 by 3 inch) pie tin with removable sides. Line the base with a double thickness of non-stick parchment paper. Cut two strips from the genoese sponge to exactly fit the dimensions of the prepared tin. Place one strip in the tin, press it down gently, and brush it with some of the reserved poaching syrup. Arrange the pear slices in a single layer on top of the sponge and spread half the custard mousse on top. Chill for 20 minutes to let the custard set slightly. Arrange the sliced figs over the partly set custard, and spread the remaining custard mousse over the figs. Brush more poaching syrup over one side of the second sponge strip and place it syrup side down on top of the custard. Cover the assembly with plastic film and press down lightly. Chill until the mousse has set — 3 to 4 hours.

Dust the surface of the sponge lightly with the icing sugar. Cover each long edge with a 2.5 cm (1 inch) wide strip of greaseproof paper and sift the cocoa powder over the exposed centre section. Slip a knife blade dipped in hot water round the edges of the assembly, then unmould it carefully. Cut the assembly into 16 slices and serve.

Passion Fruit Slices

Makes 16 slices
Working time: about 2 hours
Total time: about 6 hours (includes chilling)

Per slice:			
Calories **95**	1	egg	1
Protein **4g**	30 g	caster sugar	1 oz
Cholesterol **45mg**	30 g	plain flour	1 oz
Total fat **1g**	2 tbsp	apricot jam	2 tbsp
Saturated fat **trace**	½ tbsp	brandy or apple juice	½ tbsp
Sodium **25mg**	1½ tsp	powdered gelatine	1½ tsp
	17.5 cl	clear unsweetened apple juice	6 fl oz
		Passion fruit mousse	
	2	eggs, separated	2
	140 g	caster sugar	4½ oz
	30 g	plain flour	1 oz
	15 g	cornflour	½ oz
	30 cl	skimmed milk	½ pint
	1 tsp	pure vanilla extract	1 tsp
	10	passion fruits, halved	10
	1 tbsp	powdered gelatine	1 tbsp
	1 tbsp	fresh lemon juice	1 tbsp
	2 tbsp	unsweetened apple juice	2 tbsp
	90 g	thick Greek yogurt	3 oz

Preheat the oven to 180°C (350°F or Mark 4). Butter a 20 by 20 by 4 cm (8 by 8 by 1½ inch) baking tin and line the base with non-stick parchment paper.

Make a fatless sponge by whisking together the egg and caster sugar in a bowl set over a saucepan of simmering water on very low heat. When the mixture is thick and foamy, remove the bowl from the saucepan and continue whisking until the mixture is cool and falls from the whisk in a thick ribbon trail. Sift the flour very lightly over the surface of the whisked mixture, then fold it in gently using a large metal spoon. Pour the batter into the prepared baking tin and spread it evenly. Bake until it is springy to the touch and very slightly shrunk from the sides of the tin — 8 to 10 minutes. Carefully turn the sponge on to a wire rack and allow it to cool.

Meanwhile, make the passion fruit mousse. Beat the egg yolks with 15 g (½ oz) of the sugar in a bowl until thick, then fold in the plain flour and cornflour. Put the milk and vanilla extract into a saucepan and heat them until nearly boiling. Gradually whisk the scalding milk into the beaten egg yolks. Strain the mixture back into the saucepan and bring it to the boil, stirring constantly. Beat the egg custard well and simmer it for a further 5 minutes, while continuing to stir it. Spoon the custard into a bowl and allow it to cool a little, covering the surface closely with plastic film to prevent a skin from forming.

Spoon the flesh and seeds of the passion fruits into a nylon sieve and press them with the back of a spoon to squeeze out all the available juice. Reserve the juice and 1 teaspoon of the seeds; discard the rest.

Sprinkle the gelatine over the lemon juice and apple juice in a small bowl. Leave to soften for 2 minutes, then set the bowl over a saucepan of simmering water and stir until the gelatine has completely dissolved. Warm the passion fruit juice in a saucepan, then stir in the gelatine solution. Cool the mixture to room temperature while you make the meringue.

Put the egg whites and the remaining 125 g (4 oz) of caster sugar in a bowl set over a pan of simmering water, taking care that the bowl does not touch the water. Whisk gently until the sugar has melted, then whisk more vigorously until the mixture is stiff and glossy. Remove the meringue from the heat.

Whisk the gelatine mixture into the custard, and, when it is thick and creamy, stir in the yogurt. Stir 1 tablespoon of the meringue thoroughly into the custard, then gently fold in the rest. Keep the mousse at room temperature.

Brush almond oil or another flavourless oil over the base and sides of a 38 by 7.5 cm (15 by 3 inch) pie tin with removable sides. Line the base with a double thickness of non-stick parchment paper. Trim and cut the baked sponge to fit the base of the prepared tin and press it firmly into position.

Heat the apricot jam until liquid, pass it through a sieve, then stir in the brandy or apple juice. Brush this mixture over the surface of the sponge. Pour the fruit mousse into the tin and place it in the refrigerator until the mousse is fairly firm — about 2 hours.

Towards the end of the chilling time, make an apple jelly glaze. Dissolve the gelatine in 2 tablespoons of the clear apple juice, in the same way as described above. Heat the remaining apple juice and stir in the dissolved gelatine. Let it cool, then chill until it has thickened slightly — about 10 to 15 minutes. Stir in the reserved teaspoon of passion fruit seeds. Carefully pour the apple jelly over the mousse (the seeds may be rearranged before the jelly sets). Return the glazed mousse to the refrigerator for a further hour or two.

Slip a knife blade, dipped in hot water, round the edges of the assembly, then unmould it carefully. Cut into 16 slices and serve.

Espresso Cakes

Makes 8 cakes
Working (and total) time: about 25 minutes

Per cake:
Calories **225**
Protein **7g**
Cholesterol **120mg**
Total fat **8g**
Saturated fat **4g**
Sodium **55mg**

1	genoese sponge (recipe, page 11), 1 teaspoon of brandy added to uncooked batter	1
2 tbsp	brandy	2 tbsp
4 tbsp	very strong black coffee (not instant coffee)	4 tbsp
15 cl	liqueur-flavoured pastry cream (recipe, page 11), flavoured with brandy	¼ pint
15 g	cocoa powder	½ oz
15 g	coffee beans, finely ground	½ oz
8	chocolate coffee-bean sweets	8

Trim off the four outer crusts from the edge of the cooked sponge. Using a long, sharp knife, cut the sponge in half horizontally, making two large sheets. Combine the brandy and black coffee and, using a pastry brush, lightly paint the mixture on to the cut faces of the sponge sheets. Cut each sheet crosswise through the centre, making four rectangles in all.

Spread one third of the brandy-flavoured pastry cream over the cut surface of one of the rectangles, bringing it right up to the edges. Arrange a second rectangle, cut side down, over the cream. Spread on another third of the filling. Lay the third rectangle, cut side up, over the cream. Smooth on the last of the filling, then set the final rectangle, cut side down, on the top. Using a long, sharp knife, halve the assembly lengthwise, then cut each half crosswise into four equal pieces, to give a total of eight cakes.

Place the espresso cakes in a straight line and cover half of each one with a sheet of paper or thin card. Sift the cocoa powder over the exposed half of each cake; the layer of cocoa powder should be fairly thick or the liquid in the sponge will soak through and produce dark patches. Carefully move the paper or card to cover the cocoa topping and sift the finely ground coffee beans over the halves now exposed. Finally, decorate each espresso cake with a chocolate coffee-bean sweet.

Lime and Coconut Rum Genoese

Makes 8 slices
Working time: about 25 minutes
Total time: about 55 minutes

Per slice:
Calories **215**
Protein **6g**
Cholesterol **90mg**
Total fat **7g**
Saturated fat **3g**
Sodium **50mg**

1	genoese sponge (recipe, page 11), finely grated rind of two limes added to batter	1
3	limes, juice only	3
3½ tbsp	coconut rum or white rum	3½ tbsp
175 g	fromage frais	6 oz
175 g	plus ½ tbsp icing sugar	6 oz
	lime slices, to decorate	
	coconut shavings, briefly toasted	

Trim the four outer crusts from the edges of the sponge. Combine the juice of two of the limes with 3 tablespoons of the rum. Using a pastry brush, lightly paint the lime mixture on to the top of the sponge.

Mix the *fromage frais* with the remaining rum and the ½ tablespoon of icing sugar. Cut the sponge crosswise into three equal rectangles. Layer the rectangles, one on top of another, with the flavoured *fromage frais*, so there are three layers of sponge and two of filling.

Sift the 175 g (6 oz) of icing sugar into a bowl and stir in the remaining lime juice, and a little water if necessary, to make a glacé icing. Beat the icing until it is smooth and coats the back of a spoon. Carefully spread the icing over the top of the cake and allow to almost set. Lightly score the top into eight equal portions. Decorate each one with halved slices of lime and with toasted coconut shavings. Allow the icing to set firmly before slicing and serving.

EDITOR'S NOTE: *Use a vegetable peeler to cut coconut shavings, slicing them from the outer surface of a peeled section of fresh coconut. To toast them, put them briefly under a hot grill.*

Chocolate Mousse Layered Sponge

Makes 20 slices
Working time: about 45 minutes
Total time: about 1 hour and 25 minutes

Per slice:
Calories **90**
Protein **3g**
Cholesterol **35mg**
Total fat **3g**
Saturated fat **1g**
Sodium **40mg**

3	egg yolks	3
100 g	vanilla-flavoured caster sugar	3½ oz
4	egg whites	4
125 g	plain flour	4 oz
Chocolate mousse filling		
½ tsp	powdered gelatine	½ tsp
100 g	plain chocolate, chopped	3½ oz
100 g	low-fat ricotta cheese, sieved	3½ oz
2	egg whites	2

Preheat the oven to 180°C (350°F or Mark 4). Grease a 25 by 18 cm (10 by 7 inch) baking tin and line the base with non-stick parchment paper.

To make the sponge, put the egg yolks and three quarters of the sugar into a mixing bowl. Place the bowl over a saucepan of hot, but not boiling, water set over a low heat. Whisk the eggs and sugar together with an electric hand-held mixer until thick and very pale. Remove the bowl from the saucepan and continue whisking until the mixture is cool and falls from the whisk in a ribbon trail. In a separate bowl, using a clean whisk, beat the egg whites until stiff, sprinkle on the remaining sugar, and whisk again until the mixture becomes glossy. Sift a third of the flour over the surface of the egg yolk mixture, add a third of the whites, and gently but quickly fold them in using a large metal spoon. Add the remaining flour and egg whites in two more batches, using the same technique.

When all the ingredients are evenly combined, pour the batter into the prepared tin and bake it for 25 to 30 minutes, until the sponge is well risen, springy to the touch and very slightly shrunk from the sides of the tin. Carefully unmould the sponge on to a wire rack covered with greaseproof paper. Allow to cool for 2 or 3 minutes, then gently loosen the lining paper, but do not remove it. Place another wire rack over the bottom of the sponge and invert both racks together so the sponge is the right way up. Remove the top rack and leave the sponge to cool while preparing the filling.

Sprinkle the gelatine over 1½ tablespoons of water in a small bowl. Leave it to soften for 2 minutes, then place the bowl over a pan of simmering water and stir until the gelatine has completely dissolved. Melt the chocolate in a large heatproof bowl placed over a pan of hot, not boiling, water. Remove the bowl from the heat and, while the chocolate is still warm, gradually beat in the ricotta, keeping the mixture smooth all the time. Gradually beat the gelatine solution into the chocolate mixture. Whisk the egg whites until stiff, then lightly fold them into the mixture. Leave the mousse to set — about 30 minutes.

Using a long, sharp knife, trim the edges off the sponge and cut it in half lengthwise. Cut horizontally through each piece, to make four thin rectangles. Spread a third of the chocolate mousse filling over the cut surface of one sponge rectangle, and place another, cut side down, on top. Spread this with another third of the filling, and cover it with the third rectangle of sponge, cut side up. Repeat with the remaining filling and final layer of sponge, placed cut side down. Press the layers lightly together.

To serve, cut the assembly crosswise into 10 thin fingers, then cut across these to make 20 slices.

Chocolate Mousse and Redcurrant Boxes

Makes 12 boxes
Working time: about 1 hour and 20 minutes
Total time: about 2 hours and 30 minutes (includes chilling)

Per box:			
Calories **145**	200 g	plain chocolate	7 oz
Protein **3g**	½ tbsp	strong black coffee, cooled	½ tbsp
Cholesterol **40mg**	1	egg yolk	1
Total fat **6g**	½ tbsp	brandy	½ tbsp
Saturated fat **3g**	2	egg whites	2
Sodium **20mg**	200 g	redcurrants, topped and tailed	7 oz
	Fatless sponge		
	1	egg	1
	1	egg white	1
	60 g	caster sugar	2 oz
	60 g	plain flour	2 oz

First, make the chocolate mousse. Melt 60 g (2 oz) of the chocolate with the coffee in a large heatproof bowl over a pan of hot, but not boiling, water over low heat. Allow it to cool for a few minutes, then stir in the egg yolk and the brandy. In a separate bowl, whisk the egg whites until they are very stiff. Fold them into the chocolate mixture and allow the mousse to set in the refrigerator — about 2 hours — while you prepare the sponge and chocolate rectangles.

Preheat the oven to 180°C (350°F or Mark 4). Butter a 20 cm (8 inch) square tin and line the base with non-stick parchment paper.

For the sponge, put the egg, egg white and sugar into a mixing bowl. Place the bowl over a saucepan of hot, but not boiling, water over low heat. Whisk the eggs and sugar together by hand or with an electric hand-held mixer until it is thick and very pale. Remove the bowl from the saucepan and continue whisking until the mixture is cool and falls from the whisk in a ribbon trail. Sift the flour very lightly over the surface of the whisked mixture, then fold it in gently using a large metal spoon.

Pour the sponge mixture into the prepared tin and spread it evenly. Bake it for 20 to 25 minutes, until well risen, springy to the touch and very slightly shrunk from the sides of the tin. Carefully turn the sponge cake on to a wire rack. Loosen the baking paper but do not remove it. Place another wire rack on top of the paper, then invert both racks together so that the sponge is right side up on top of the paper. Remove the top rack and allow the sponge to cool.

Grease a 30 by 23 cm (12 by 9 inch) square-cornered shallow baking tin and line the base with greaseproof paper. Melt the remaining chocolate in a heatproof bowl set over a pan of hot water. Pour it into the prepared tin, spread it evenly with a metal spatula and leave it to set in a cool place — about 30 minutes. Cut the chocolate *(page 12)* into 36 rectangles, each measuring 7.5 by 2.5 cm (3 by 1 inch). Cut 12 of the rectangles in half crosswise, to make end pieces for the chocolate boxes.

Trim the crusts off the sponge and slice it into twelve 7.5 by 3 cm (3 by 1¼ inch) fingers. Using a metal spatula, spread a little of the mousse along the four sides of each sponge finger. Form little chocolate boxes by gently pressing the long and short chocolate rectangles against the covered sides of the sponge fingers. Fill the boxes with the remaining mousse, and top them with a layer of redcurrants. Carefully transfer the boxes to serving plates.

EDITOR'S NOTE: *Raspberries or small strawberries may be used instead of redcurrants.*

White Chocolate Coffee Rolls

Makes 16 rolls
Working time: about 1 hour
Total time: about 2 hours (includes chilling)

Per roll:
Calories **215**
Protein **5g**
Cholesterol **40mg**
Total fat **10g**
Saturated fat **6g**
Sodium **40mg**

1 tbsp	powdered gelatine	1 tbsp
15 cl	strong black coffee, cooled	¼ pint
1 tsp	Tia Maria	1 tsp
250 g	fromage frais	8 oz
1	genoese sponge (recipe, page 11), 2 teaspoons of very strong black coffee added to uncooked batter	1
300 g	white chocolate	10 oz
30 g	plain chocolate	1 oz

Sprinkle the gelatine over 2 tablespoons of the cold black coffee in a small bowl, leave it to soften for 2 minutes, then set the bowl over a saucepan of simmering water and stir until the gelatine has completely dissolved. Blend the remaining coffee with the Tia Maria and *fromage frais* in a food processor or blender until smooth. Add the gelatine solution and process for a further 20 seconds. Refrigerate the coffee cream filling until it has set — 1 to 1 ½ hours.

Using a long, sharp knife, cut through the genoese sponge horizontally to make two thin sheets of cake. Trim off any dry crusts. Cut each sheet in half lengthwise, then cut each strip crosswise into four, to give a total of sixteen 10 by 7.5 cm (4 by 3 inch) rectangles. Place each rectangle between two sheets of non-stick parchment paper and roll it a little with a rolling pin; this will flatten the sponge and prevent it from cracking when it is rolled up with the filling.

Spread the cut side of each sponge rectangle with an even layer — about 5 mm (¼ inch) deep — of the coffee filling, keeping it away from the edges. Roll up each rectangle, starting from a short side, to make a tightly-rolled cake.

To ice the rolls, melt the white chocolate in a heatproof bowl set over a saucepan of simmering water. Place a roll on a metal spatula, seam-side down. Hold it over the bowl of white chocolate, and spoon the chocolate over the roll, covering it completely. Place the iced roll on a sheet of parchment paper. Repeat until all the rolls have been coated.

Melt the plain chocolate over hot water as described for the white chocolate above, and spoon it into a greaseproof paper piping bag *(page 13)*. Decorate the rolls with zigzags of fine chocolate piping. Allow the chocolate to set before serving.

Chocolate-Orange Roulades

Makes 16 roulades
Working time: about 1 hour
Total time: about 1 hour and 30 minutes

Per roulade:
Calories **195**
Protein **4g**
Cholesterol **60mg**
Total fat **8g**
Saturated fat **5g**
Sodium **25mg**

300 g	plain chocolate	10 oz
1	egg yolk	1
1 tsp	Grand Marnier, Cointreau or other orange-flavoured liqueur	1 tsp
2	egg whites	2
1	genoese sponge (recipe, page 11), made with 30 g (1 oz) of cocoa powder substituted for 30 g (1 oz) of flour	1
15 g	hazelnuts, toasted and skinned (page 29), chopped	½ oz

Melt 60 g (2 oz) of the chocolate in a heatproof bowl over a saucepan of simmering water. Allow it to cool slightly, then stir in the egg yolk and Grand Marnier. In a separate bowl, whisk the egg whites until they are very stiff, then fold them into the chocolate. Refrigerate the mousse until it has set — about 30 minutes.

Using a long serrated knife, cut the genoese sponge in half horizontally to make two thin sheets. Trim off any dry crusts. Cut each sheet in half lengthwise, then cut each strip crosswise into four, to give a total of sixteen 10 by 7.5 cm (4 by 3 inch) rectangles. Place each rectangle between two sheets of non-stick parchment paper and roll it a little with a rolling pin; this will flatten the sponge and prevent it from cracking when it is rolled up with the filling.

Spread the cut surface of each rectangle with an even layer of chocolate mousse about 5 mm (¼ inch) thick; do not spread the mousse right up to the edges of the sponge. Working from a short edge, roll up each rectangle into a small tight roll.

Melt the remaining chocolate in a bowl over hot water. Place a roulade, seam-side down, on a metal spatula. Hold it over the bowl and spoon the melted chocolate over the roulade. Place the coated roll on a sheet of non-stick parchment paper and sprinkle it with chopped hazelnuts. Coat the remaining roulades in the same way and allow them to set before serving. When cool they will lift easily from the parchment paper.

Gooseberry-Meringue Sandwich Slices

Makes 10 slices
Working time: about 1 hour
Total time: about 1 hour and 50 minutes

Per slice:
Calories **210**
Protein **3g**
Cholesterol **60mg**
Total fat **8g**
Saturated fat **4g**
Sodium **120mg**

75 g	unsalted butter	2½ oz
75 g	caster sugar	2½ oz
2	egg yolks	2
1 tsp	pure vanilla extract	1 tsp
125 g	plain flour	4 oz
1 tsp	baking powder	1 tsp
10 cl	skimmed milk	3½ fl oz
Meringue topping		
2	egg whites	2
90 g	caster sugar	3 oz
Gooseberry filling		
500 g	green gooseberries, topped and tailed, halved	1 lb
100 g	caster sugar	3½ oz
½ tsp	ground cinnamon	½ tsp
1 tbsp	arrowroot	1 tbsp

Preheat the oven to 180°C (350°F or Mark 4). Line the base of a 30 by 20 by 4 cm (12 by 8 by 1½ inch) tin with non-stick parchment paper long enough to stand 4 cm (1½ inches) above the rim on the two short sides; this will ease removal of the cooked cake base.

Cream the butter and sugar together in a bowl until pale and fluffy. Add the egg yolks and vanilla and gradually blend them into the butter and sugar mixture; add 1 tablespoon of the flour if the mixture begins to curdle. Sift the remaining flour with the baking powder and fold into the mixture alternately with the milk. Mix to a smooth dropping consistency and spread the mixture evenly over the base of the lined tin.

For the meringue topping, whisk the egg whites until they form peaks. Add the sugar a tablespoon at a time, whisking constantly after each addition until the mixture is again stiff and glossy. Pile the meringue on top of the sponge mixture and spread it almost to the edges of the tin. Bake until the meringue is lightly browned and firm to the touch — about 35 minutes. Using the paper "handles", ease the whole meringue cake on to a wire rack and cool to room temperature.

Meanwhile, make the filling. Put the gooseberries into a non-reactive saucepan with 2 tablespoons of water. Stir in the sugar and cinnamon, and cook the berries very gently until they are tender but not mushy — 10 to 15 minutes. Remove the gooseberries with a slotted spoon and set them aside. Reserve 4 tablespoons of the juice. In a small bowl, blend the arrowroot with 1 tablespoon of water and stir in the reserved juice. Return this mixture to the pan and cook gently until it begins to thicken. Add the gooseberries and cook until the juice is clear and thick. Let the filling cool to room temperature — about 45 minutes.

Using a sharp knife, trim the edges of the cooled meringue-sponge and cut it in half lengthwise. Spread the gooseberry filling evenly over the meringue topping of one half of the cake. Carefully place the other half — meringue-side up — on top of the gooseberries and press it down gently. Cut the cake into 10 slices and serve soon after assembling.

EDITOR'S NOTE: *Frozen gooseberries may be used instead of fresh. There is no need to thaw them first; simply increase their cooking time in the sugar syrup to 20 to 25 minutes.*

Coconut Meringue Fingers

Makes about 36 fingers
Working time: about 30 minutes
Total time: about 1 hour and 30 minutes

Per finger:
Calories **25**
Protein **trace**
Cholesterol **0mg**
Total fat **1g**
Saturated fat **trace**
Sodium **5mg**

2	egg whites	2
125 g	vanilla-flavoured caster sugar	4 oz
60 g	desiccated coconut	2 oz

Preheat the oven to 130°C (250°F or Mark ½). Line two baking sheets with non-stick parchment paper.

Put the egg whites and sugar in a large, heatproof bowl. Set the bowl over a pan of simmering water, taking care that the bottom of the bowl does not touch the water, and whisk with an electric hand-held mixer until the mixture forms soft peaks — about 5 minutes. Remove the bowl from the heat and continue whisking at high speed until the meringue is stiff and glossy.

Using a metal spoon, lightly fold in all but 2 tablespoons of the coconut. Spoon the mixture into a piping bag fitted with a 1 cm (½ inch) plain nozzle and pipe out straight lines about 10 cm (4 inches) long on the prepared baking sheets. Sprinkle the remaining coconut over the tops of the fingers, then bake the fingers until they are crisp and dry but still white on the outside — about 1 hour. The meringue will still be slightly moist in the centre. Carefully transfer the fingers to a wire rack to cool.

EDITOR'S NOTE: *These fingers may be stored in an airtight container for four to five days.*

Chocolate-Dipped Meringue Fingers

Makes 60 fingers
Working time: about 35 minutes
Total time: about 2 hours

Per finger:
Calories **35**
Protein **trace**
Cholesterol **0mg**
Total fat **2g**
Saturated fat **1g**
Sodium **10mg**

2	egg whites	2
125 g	caster sugar	4 oz
1 tbsp	cocoa powder	1 tbsp
½ tsp	grated orange rind, thoroughly dried on kitchen paper	½ tsp
150 g	plain chocolate	5 oz
150 g	white chocolate	5 oz

Preheat the oven to 130°C (250°F or Mark ½). Line two baking sheets with non-stick parchment paper.

Whisk the egg whites until they form soft peaks. Add half the sugar and continue whisking until the mixture is stiff and glossy. Using a metal spoon, gently fold in the remaining sugar. Divide the stiffly beaten whites into two equal parts. Flavour one half with the cocoa powder and the other with the orange rind, folding the latter in very gently so as not to "break" the meringue.

Transfer one of the meringue mixtures to a piping bag fitted with a 1 cm (½ inch) plain nozzle. Pipe 7.5 cm (3 inch) fingers, spaced at least 2.5 cm (1 inch) apart on to one of the prepared baking sheets. Repeat the process with the second batch of meringue. Bake the fingers until they are completely dry — about 1 hour — then transfer them to wire racks to cool.

Melt the plain chocolate with 4 tablespoons of water in a heatproof bowl set over a pan of simmering water. Half-ice the orange-flavoured fingers by dipping them at an angle into the melted chocolate. Leave them to set on a sheet of non-stick parchment paper. Meanwhile, melt the white chocolate and coat the cocoa-flavoured fingers in the same way.

EDITOR'S NOTE: *Meringue fingers may be stored in an airtight tin in a cool, dry place for several days.*

A Trio of Meringues

Makes 24 meringues
Working time: about 1 hour
Total time: about 4 hours

*Per plain
meringue:*
Calories **80**
Protein **2g**
Cholesterol **0mg**
Total fat **2g**
Saturated fat **1g**
Sodium **60mg**

4	egg whites	4
250 g	caster sugar	8 oz
45 g	desiccated coconut, lightly toasted	1½ oz
30 g	raspberries, puréed and sieved	1 oz
30 g	plain chocolate, finely grated	1 oz
30 g	shelled walnuts, finely chopped	1 oz
Lemon-cheese filling		
250 g	low-fat curd cheese	8 oz
2	lemons, finely grated rind only	2
30 g	caster sugar	1 oz

*Per coconut
meringue:*
Calories **95**
Protein **2g**
Cholesterol **0mg**
Total fat **4g**
Saturated fat **3g**
Sodium **60mg**

*Per raspberry
meringue:*
Calories **80**
Protein **1g**
Cholesterol **0mg**
Total fat **2g**
Saturated fat **1g**
Sodium **60mg**

Preheat the oven to 100°C (200°F or Mark ¼). Line three baking sheets with non-stick parchment paper.

In a large clean bowl, whisk the egg whites until they are stiff but not dry. Gradually whisk in the caster sugar, a little at a time, whisking constantly between each addition until the meringue is very stiff and shiny.

Put one third of the meringue into a piping bag fitted with a 12-point 1 cm (½ inch) star nozzle. Put another third of the meringue into a small bowl and mix in 30 g (1 oz) of the toasted coconut, then spoon it into a piping bag fitted with a 1.5 cm (⅝ inch) plain nozzle. Fold the raspberry purée into the remaining meringue, then spoon it into a piping bag fitted with a seven-point 1 cm (½ inch) star nozzle.

Pipe the plain meringue in a continuous spiral pattern to form twelve 6 cm (2½ inch) lengths on one lined baking sheet; pipe the mixture in arcs that increase in size towards the centre and decrease towards the end. Pipe the coconut meringue in 16 rounded mounds, about 5 cm (2 inches) in diameter, on the second baking sheet. Finally, pipe the raspberry-flavoured meringue on to the third sheet to form 20 whirls about 5 cm (2 inches) in diameter. Bake the meringues until they are crisp and dry: the coconut ones need about 2 hours, the others from 2½ to 3 hours. If they begin to brown before they are crisp, lower or turn off the oven. Allow the meringues to cool on the baking sheets before removing them from the paper.

For the filling, beat the curd cheese in a bowl with the lemon rind and sugar until the mixture is smooth. Just before serving the meringues, sandwich them together in matching pairs with the lemon cheese. Sprinkle the plain meringues with the grated chocolate, the coconut meringues with the remaining 15 g (½ oz) of toasted coconut, and the raspberry meringues with the chopped walnuts.

EDITOR'S NOTE: *To toast coconut, heat it under the grill for a minute or two, turning it frequently with a spoon until it turns golden-brown.*

Chestnut Mocha Mountains

Makes 10 mountains
Working time: about 1 hour and 30 minutes
Total time: about 6 hours

Per mountain:
Calories **200**
Protein **3g**
Cholesterol **0mg**
Total fat **4g**
Saturated fat **2g**
Sodium **50mg**

3	egg whites	3
175 g	caster sugar	6 oz
1 tbsp	cocoa powder	1 tbsp
2 tsp	very finely ground coffee beans	2 tsp
450 g	fresh chestnuts, peeled (page 51)	15 oz
½	vanilla pod, split	½
30 cl	skimmed milk	½ pint
100 g	light brown sugar	3½ oz
2 to 3 tbsp	brandy or dark rum	2 to 3 tbsp
½ tsp	finely grated orange rind	½ tsp
45 g	plain chocolate	1½ oz
2	oranges, segmented (page 41) and coarsely chopped	2
8 cl	plain low-fat yogurt	3 fl oz

Preheat the oven to 100°C (200°F or Mark ¼), and line a baking sheet with non-stick parchment paper.

Put the egg whites and caster sugar in a large, heat-proof bowl. Set the bowl over a pan of simmering water, taking care that the bottom of the bowl does not touch the water, and stir the mixture with a whisk until the sugar has dissolved and the egg whites are hot — about 5 minutes. Remove the bowl from the heat and whisk the mixture vigorously until peaks begin to form. Stir in the cocoa powder and ground coffee beans, and whisk again, briefly, until the meringue is stiff and glossy.

Transfer the meringue to a piping bag fitted with a 1 cm (½ inch) plain nozzle and pipe it in two stages, which will be easier than in one. Pipe 10 closed-up coils of meringue, each about 7.5 cm (3 inches) in diameter, on to the prepared baking sheet. These form the bases of the meringue cases. To make the walls which will enclose the filling, either pipe two rings of meringue round the edge of each coil, or fit the piping bag with a 1 cm (½ inch) star nozzle and pipe small shell shapes *(as illustrated here)*, about 1 cm (½ inch) high, all the way round the edge of each base. Cook the meringue nests for about 4 hours until they are firm to the touch and can be easily lifted from the paper. Transfer them to a wire rack to cool.

Meanwhile, make the chestnut filling. Put the peeled chestnuts, vanilla pod and milk in a heavy-bottomed saucepan. Bring to the boil, then reduce the heat and simmer gently until the chestnuts are very soft — 25 to 30 minutes. Remove the chestnuts with a slotted spoon. Remove and rinse the vanilla pod. Force the chestnuts through a sieve or reduce them to a rough powder in a food processor.

Dissolve the light brown sugar in a saucepan with 5 tablespoons of water. Add the vanilla pod, and boil until the syrup is thick and lightly caramelized — about 3 minutes. Remove the vanilla pod and cool the syrup

for a minute before beating it into the powdered chestnuts. Add the brandy to taste, but do not allow the chestnut purée to become too sticky — you should be able to rice or pipe it easily. Stir in the orange rind.

Melt the chocolate in a heatproof bowl set over a saucepan of simmering water. Brush a little of the melted chocolate over the base of each meringue case and leave to harden. Mix the oranges and yogurt together and spoon into the cases.

Make a mound of chestnut vermicelli on top of each meringue by pressing the purée through a potato ricer. Drop the strands of chestnut directly into the nests from the press, using a small knife to cut the strands when enough mixture has been pressed through. Alternatively, use an icing bag and small plain nozzle, piping the purée directly into each nest in a winding pattern until a mound is formed.

The nests will keep for a few hours. If not serving them immediately, cover them lightly with plastic film to prevent the chestnut from becoming too dry.

Chocolate Meringue Leaves

Makes 12 leaves
Working time: about 1 hour and 15 minutes
Total time: about 3 hours and 15 minutes

Per leaf:
Calories **100**
Protein **3g**
Cholesterol **20mg**
Total fat **4g**
Saturated fat **2g**
Sodium **15mg**

2	egg whites	2
125 g	caster sugar	4 oz
75 g	plain chocolate, 30 g (1 oz) grated	2½ oz
15 cl	chocolate-flavoured pastry cream (recipe, page 11)	¼ pint

Preheat the oven to 100°C (200°F or Mark ¼). Cut a leaf-shaped template — about 9 cm (3½ inches) long and 7.5 cm (3 inches) wide — from a piece of card. Cut sheets of non-stick parchment paper to fit two baking sheets. Draw six leaves on each sheet by tracing round the template with a pencil; leave at least 2.5 cm (1 inch) between leaves. Invert the papers and press them into greased baking sheets.

Whisk the egg whites until they form soft peaks. Still whisking, add the sugar a little at a time — ensuring the mixture is stiff and glossy after each addition of sugar before adding more. Using a metal spoon, lightly fold in the 30 g (1 oz) of grated chocolate.

Transfer the mixture to a piping bag fitted with a 5 mm (¼ inch) plain nozzle, and pipe 12 leaf shapes on to the prepared baking sheets *(box, right)*. Bake the leaves until they are dry and will lift off the paper — 2 to 3 hours. They will still be a little soft in the centre as the chocolate prevents them from hardening completely. Let them cool on the greaseproof paper.

Meanwhile, make the chocolate filigree leaves. On a piece of white card, draw a leaf shape, about 2.5 cm (1 inch) shorter and narrower than the meringue template, and cut three 45 by 15 cm (18 by 6 inch) rectangles of greaseproof paper. Melt the remaining 45 g (1½ oz) of chocolate in a heatproof bowl set over a saucepan of simmering water. Make a greaseproof paper piping bag, fill it with the melted chocolate, and snip off the tip of the bag *(page 13)*. Using the card as a tracing guide, pipe four chocolate filigree leaves on to each rectangle of paper as demonstrated below. Leave the chocolate leaves to set.

To serve, fill each meringue leaf with chocolate-flavoured pastry cream. Carefully peel the backing paper away from the filigree leaves and gently lay one on top of each meringue.

Chocolate Filigree Leaves

FINE-PIPING THE LEAVES. Place a rectangle of greaseproof paper over the tracing guide and hold it firmly with one hand. Trace the outline of the leaf with a fine line of piped chocolate. Then, starting at the tip, fill in the centre of the leaf by piping back and forth in a continuous pattern of squiggles. Reposition the guide before piping the next leaf.

Making Meringue Leaves

1 *PIPING THE OUTLINES. Twist the top of the piping bag closed and, exerting a firm steady pressure, pipe out the meringue to form leaf outlines, following the pencilled guidelines.*

2 *FILLING IN THE CENTRES. Starting at the pointed end of each leaf, move the piping bag back and forth horizontally to fill in the outlines with rows of evenly piped meringue. Pipe a short stem on to the base of each leaf.*

3 *COMPLETING THE LEAVES. Pipe a series of dots round the outside of each leaf, to form a border. Pipe a second stem on top of the first.*

Hazelnut Scallops with Chocolate Icing

Makes 20 scallops
Working time: about 1 hour
Total time: about 8 hours and 30 minutes

Per scallop:
Calories **90**
Protein **1g**
Cholesterol **0mg**
Total fat **3g**
Saturated fat **1g**
Sodium **10mg**

3	egg whites	3
175 g	caster sugar	6 oz
90 g	shelled hazelnuts, toasted and skinned (page 29), ground	3 oz
60 g	plain chocolate	2 oz
1½ tsp	strong black coffee, cooled	1½ tsp
7 g	unsalted butter	¼ oz
30 g	icing sugar	1 oz
1 tbsp	frangelico or amaretto liqueur	1 tbsp

Preheat the oven to 100°C (200°F or Mark ¼). Line a large baking sheet with non-stick parchment paper.

Whisk the egg whites until they are very stiff. Beat in the sugar, a little at a time, whisking well between each addition until the meringue is stiff and glossy. Fold in the hazelnuts with a metal spoon.

Transfer the meringue to a piping bag fitted with a 2 cm (¾ inch) star nozzle, and pipe 40 scallop shapes on to the lined baking sheet. Bake for 2½ hours, or until the meringues feel firm to the touch and come away from the paper easily. Turn off the oven but leave the meringues inside until they are cold and completely dry — about 4 hours, or overnight.

Melt the chocolate with the coffee in a heatproof bowl set over a pan of simmering water. Stir in the butter. Sift in the icing sugar and beat well. Allow to cool briefly, then stir in the liqueur. Leave a few minutes more, until thickened slightly. Sandwich meringues in pairs with the icing, and dip the ends in the icing. Place the scallops on a sheet of non-stick parchment paper until the icing has set — about 1 hour.

EDITOR'S NOTE: *Frangelico is an Italian liqueur made from hazelnuts; amaretto is made from almonds.*

Walnut Meringues with Rose-Water Cream and Strawberries

Makes 10 meringues
Working time: about 30 minutes
Total time: about 7 hours

Per meringue:
Calories **155**
Protein **2g**
Cholesterol **15mg**
Total fat **8g**
Saturated fat **3g**
Sodium **20mg**

3	egg whites	3
175 g	caster sugar	6 oz
45 g	shelled walnuts, chopped and lightly toasted	1½ oz
15 cl	whipping cream	¼ pint
¼ tsp	rose-water	¼ tsp
350 g	strawberries, hulled and thinly sliced	12 oz

Preheat the oven to 100°C (200°F or Mark ¼). Line a baking sheet with non-stick parchment paper.

Whisk the egg whites until the mixture is so stiff that it clings to the whisk when it is held upside down. Add the caster sugar, a little at a time, whisking constantly after each addition until the mixture is again stiff and glossy. With a metal spoon, fold in the chopped walnuts and half of the rose-water.

Transfer the mixture to a piping bag fitted with a 2 cm (¾ inch) star nozzle, and pipe 20 small whirls about 5 cm (2 inches) in diameter on to the prepared baking sheet. Bake the meringues for 2½ hours until they can be lifted easily off the paper, then turn off the oven but leave the meringues inside until they are cold and completely dry — about 4 hours, or overnight.

Just before serving, whip the cream in a bowl, add the remaining ⅛ teaspoon of rose-water, and gently fold in the sliced strawberries. Sandwich pairs of meringues together with this filling.

EDITOR'S NOTE: *To toast walnuts, put them under a hot grill for about a minute, shaking frequently.*

Pistachio Meringues

Makes 12 meringues
Working time: about 30 minutes
Total time: about 7 hours

Per meringue:			
Calories **135**	3	egg whites	3
Protein **2g**	175 g	caster sugar	6 oz
Cholesterol **15mg**	60 g	shelled pistachio nuts, skinned,	2 oz
Total fat **7g**		15 g (½ oz) chopped, remainder cut	
Saturated fat **3g**		into slivers	
Sodium **20mg**	15 cl	whipping cream	¼ pint
	1	kiwi fruit, peeled and sliced,	1
		slices quartered	

Preheat the oven to 100°C (200°F or Mark ¼). Line two baking sheets with non-stick parchment paper.

Whisk the egg whites until the mixture is so stiff that it clings to the whisk when it is held upside down.

Gradually add the sugar, a little at a time, whisking constantly after each addition until the mixture is again stiff and glossy. With a metal spoon, gently fold in the slivered pistachio nuts. Transfer the mixture to a piping bag fitted with a 2.5 cm (1 inch) plain nozzle and pipe 24 small meringues, each about 5 cm (2 inches) in diameter, on to the prepared baking sheets.

Bake the meringues for 2½ hours, until they will move easily on the paper. Turn off the oven and allow the meringues to rest in the oven until they are cold and completely dry — about 4 hours, or overnight.

Just before serving, whip the cream in a bowl and use it to sandwich the meringues together in pairs; for a decorative effect, pipe the cream through a star nozzle. Decorate the meringues with the chopped pistachio nuts and kiwi quarters. Serve immediately.

EDITOR'S NOTE: *To skin pistachio nuts, blanch them in boiling water for 1 minute, drain them and rub them briskly in a towel until they have shed their skins.*

Cherry-Chocolate Meringue Nests

Makes 8 nests
Working time: about 45 minutes
Total time: about 6 hours

Per nest:
Calories **145**
Protein **2g**
Cholesterol **0mg**
Total fat **3g**
Saturated fat **2g**
Sodium **15mg**

2	egg whites	2
125 g	caster sugar	4 oz
45 g	plain chocolate	1 ½ oz
1 tbsp	kirsch	1 tbsp
150 g	fromage frais	5 oz
150 g	cherries, stoned and halved	5 oz
3 tbsp	cherry jam	3 tbsp
1 tsp	arrowroot	1 tsp

Preheat the oven to 100°C (200°F or Mark ¼). Line a baking sheet with non-stick parchment paper and, using an oval cutter as a guide, pencil eight 7.5 by 5 cm (3 by 2 inch) ovals on to the paper; leave at least 2.5 cm (1 inch) between ovals. Turn the paper over so that the marks face downwards.

Put the egg whites and sugar into a large bowl over a pan of simmering water, taking care that the bowl does not touch the water. Stir the mixture with a whisk until the sugar has dissolved and the egg whites are hot — about 4 minutes — then whisk more vigorously until the meringue is stiff and glossy.

Spoon the meringue into a piping bag fitted with a 1 cm (½ inch) star nozzle, and make bases for the nests by filling in the pencilled ovals on the baking paper with piped coils of meringue. To make the sides of the nests, pipe two layers — one on top of the other — round the edge of each base. Bake the nests until they are crisp and dry, but not brown — 5 to 6 hours. Carefully transfer them to a wire rack to cool.

Melt the chocolate in a heatproof bowl set over a pan of simmering water. Carefully paint the base inside each nest with a thin layer of melted chocolate.

Beat the kirsch into the *fromage frais* and, when the chocolate has set, spoon it into the nests. Top the flavoured *fromage frais* with the halved cherries.

In a small, non-reactive saucepan, heat the jam with 2 tablespoons of water until liquid. Sieve the melted jam to remove any solids, then stir in the arrowroot. Return the mixture to the pan and bring it to the boil, stirring constantly. Remove the pan from the heat and allow the glaze to thicken before brushing it carefully over the cherries in each nest.

Fruit-Filled Meringue Baskets

Makes 8 baskets
Working time: about 45 minutes
Total time: about 3 hours and 45 minutes

Per basket:	90 g	caster sugar	3 oz
Calories **85**	30 g	light brown sugar	1 oz
Protein **1g**	2	egg whites	2
Cholesterol **0mg**		**Fruit filling**	
Total fat **0g**	90 g	fresh raspberries	3 oz
Saturated fat **0g**	1	kiwi fruit, peeled, halved lengthwise and sliced	1
Sodium **15mg**	60 g	green seedless grapes, halved	2 oz
	125 g	fresh strawberries, hulled and sliced	4 oz
	2 tbsp	kirsch or dry white wine	2 tbsp

Heat the oven to 100°C (200°F or Mark ¼). Line a large baking sheet with non-stick parchment paper and pencil eight 6 cm (2½ inch) squares on the paper, spaced at least 2.5 cm (1 inch) apart. Turn the paper over so that the marks face downwards.

Sift together the caster sugar and brown sugar. Whisk the egg whites until they form soft peaks. Continue whisking while gradually adding the combined sugars, a tablespoon at a time; the mixture should be stiff and glossy after each addition of sugar. Transfer the meringue to a piping bag fitted with a 1 cm (½ inch) star nozzle. First pipe round the edge of each outlined square on the baking paper, then pipe back and forth across the squares to make bases for the baskets. Make sides for the baskets by piping a border, two layers high, round the edge of each base. Complete the baskets with a meringue "star" at each corner.

Cook the meringues until they are completely dry and will lift easily off the paper — 2½ to 3 hours. Cool them on a wire rack.

Put the raspberries, kiwi slices, grape halves and strawberry slices in a bowl and stir in the kirsch or wine. Leave the fruit to stand for at least 30 minutes, stirring occasionally. Just before serving, arrange the fruit decoratively in the meringue baskets.

Spicy Pear Roulade

Serves 18
Working time: about 1 hour
Total time: about 8 hours (includes soaking and proving)

Calories **110**
Protein **2g**
Cholesterol **15mg**
Total fat **3g**
Saturated fat **trace**
Sodium **60mg**

250 g	strong plain flour	8 oz
½ tsp	salt	½ tsp
5	cardamom pods, husks removed and seeds ground	5
15 g	fresh yeast, or ½ tsp dried yeast	½ oz
30 g	light brown sugar	1 oz
6 tbsp	skimmed milk, tepid	6 tbsp
1	egg, lightly beaten	1
1 tbsp	walnut or safflower oil	1 tbsp
1 tsp	caster sugar	1 tsp
	Spicy pear filling	
60 g	fresh crumbs from dark pumpernickel bread or gingerbread	2 oz
2 tbsp	calvados or dark rum	2 tbsp
2 tbsp	dark muscovado sugar	2 tbsp
1 tbsp	clear honey	1 tbsp
1 tbsp	cocoa powder	1 tbsp
1 tbsp	mixed spice	1 tbsp
45 g	shelled pecan nuts, roughly chopped	1½ oz
175 g	dried pears, soaked for at least 4 hours, drained and roughly chopped	6 oz

Sift the flour, salt and cardamom together into a warm mixing bowl. Crumble the fresh yeast and mix it with 1 teaspoon of the light brown sugar and 5 tablespoons of the milk. If using dried yeast, activate it according to the manufacturer's instructions. Add 60 g (2 oz) of the flour mixture to the yeast and stir with a fork to form a soft paste. Set this aside in a warm place to rise for about 30 minutes.

Form a hollow in the remaining flour mixture and add the risen yeast, egg, oil and remaining light brown sugar. Using a wooden spoon, blend the liquid ingredients well, then gradually draw in the flour. When the dough becomes too stiff to mix easily with the spoon, use your hands. Turn the dough on to a floured surface and knead it until smooth, elastic and not too sticky — about 10 minutes. Transfer the dough to a lightly oiled bowl and cover with a piece of plastic film, then put the bowl in a warm place until the dough has doubled in bulk — about 1½ hours.

Knock back the proved dough, turn it out on to a floured surface and knead it for 2 to 3 minutes. Sprinkle more flour on to the work surface and the dough, then roll out the dough to form a rectangle about 38 by 30 cm (15 by 12 inches).

For the filling, moisten the crumbs with the calvados or rum and stir in the muscovado sugar. Spread the crumbs over the rectangle of dough, extending right to the edge on three sides but leaving a margin of 2.5 cm (1 inch) free of filling along one long edge. Dribble the honey over the crumbs, sift on the cocoa and mixed spice and sprinkle on the pecans. Arrange the pears in three rows parallel with the filling-free edge, stopping the rows 2.5 cm (1 inch) from the edge of the crumbs. Roll up the dough, starting with the long side which has been coated to the edge. Seal the ends by pressing them together. Place the roll, seam side down, on a lightly buttered baking sheet, tucking down the sealed ends.

Preheat the oven to 180°C (350°F or Mark 4), allowing the roulade to prove a little, loosely covered with plastic film, while the oven is warming. Just before baking, dissolve the caster sugar in the remaining milk and brush this over the dough as a glaze. Bake the roulade until it is golden-brown and sounds slightly hollow when tapped — 35 to 45 minutes. Cool it on a wire rack; for a soft crust, wrap it in a clean cloth while it is still warm. Slice shortly before serving.

SUGGESTED ACCOMPANIMENT: *soured cream or Greek yogurt.*

Brioche Peaches

Makes 10 peaches
Working time: about 1 hour and 30 minutes
Total time: about 7 hours and 45 minutes
(includes rising and cooling)

Per peach:
Calories **225**
Protein **5g**
Cholesterol **65mg**
Total fat **8g**
Saturated fat **4g**
Sodium **40mg**

15 g	fresh yeast, or ½ tsp dried yeast	½ oz
3 tbsp	skimmed milk, tepid	3 tbsp
275 g	strong plain flour	9 oz
15 g	caster sugar	½ oz
⅛ tsp	salt	⅛ tsp
2	eggs, beaten	2
90 g	unsalted butter, softened	3 oz
	angelica, cut into 20 small leaves	
	caster sugar, to decorate	
Almond cream filling		
½ tsp	pure almond extract	½ tsp
1	egg white	1
45 g	caster sugar	1½ oz
100 g	fromage frais	3½ oz
Apricot-raspberry glaze		
30 g	caster sugar	1 oz
2 tbsp	white rum	2 tbsp
2 tbsp	apricot jam	2 tbsp
1 tbsp	raspberry jam	1 tbsp

To make the brioche dough, dissolve the fresh yeast in the tepid milk, or activate the dried yeast according to the manufacturer's instructions. Sift the flour, sugar and salt into a mixing bowl and make a well in the centre. Pour the yeast liquid into the flour and add the eggs. Beat the ingredients together well with a wooden spoon to form a soft dough.

Transfer the dough to a lightly floured surface and knead it for 10 to 15 minutes by lifting it and slapping it down on the work surface until it becomes firm and elastic. Work the butter, a little at a time, into the dough. Place the dough in a clean bowl. Cover the bowl with plastic film, then refrigerate the dough for 5 hours, to allow it to rise very slowly.

Lightly butter two large baking sheets. Turn the risen dough on to a floured surface and knock it back to its original size. Knead lightly for 2 to 3 minutes, until smooth. Shape the dough into a long sausage and cut it into 20 equal-sized pieces. Shape each piece into a neat round and place on the buttered baking sheets, spaced well apart. Flatten each round slightly, then cover the baking sheets with plastic film. Leave in a warm place for about 30 minutes, until the rounds have doubled in size. Meanwhile, preheat the oven to 220°C (425°F or Mark 7).

Remove the plastic film and bake the brioches for 15 minutes, until they are well risen, golden-brown, and sound hollow when tapped on the base. Remove them to wire racks to cool.

Meanwhile, make the almond cream filling. Put the almond extract, egg white and caster sugar in a small bowl and place the bowl over a saucepan of gently simmering water — the bottom of the bowl must not touch the water. Whisk the egg white and sugar until very thick and glossy. Remove from the heat and continue to whisk the mixture until it is cool. Very gradually whisk the *fromage frais* into the meringue. Refrigerate until needed.

Using a small pointed knife, cut out a small cone shape from the base of each brioche to make a hollow. Fill the hollows with the almond cream and sandwich pairs of brioches together to form peaches. Place the peaches on wire racks.

To make the glaze, put the caster sugar into a small saucepan with 4 tablespoons of cold water. Heat gently over a low heat, stirring until every crystal of sugar is dissolved. Bring to the boil and boil for 30 seconds, then remove the saucepan from the heat and stir in the rum. Brush the hot rum syrup over the peaches. Heat the apricot and raspberry jams in separate saucepans, until boiling, then sieve them to remove any solids. Brush the apricot jam over the peaches to coat them completely and "blush" each one with a pastry brush dipped in the raspberry jam.

Sift a little caster sugar over the peaches and decorate each one with two angelica leaves. Place in paper cases for serving.

Poppy Seed Babas

Makes 24 babas
Working time: about 1 hour and 15 minutes
Total time: about 3 hours (includes rising)

Per baba:			
Calories **145**	30 g	fresh yeast, or 1 tsp dried yeast	1 oz
Protein **3g**	17.5 cl	skimmed milk, tepid	6 fl oz
Cholesterol **25mg**	75 g	light brown sugar	2½ oz
Total fat **5g**	300 g	strong plain flour	10 oz
Saturated fat **2g**	2	eggs, separated	2
Sodium **95mg**	1 tsp	pure vanilla extract	1 tsp
	½	lemon, grated rind only	½
	⅛ tsp	powdered saffron	⅛ tsp
	1 tbsp	vodka	1 tbsp
	¼ tsp	salt	¼ tsp
	60 g	semolina, preferably coarsely ground	2 oz

75 g	unsalted butter, melted	2½ oz
30 g	candied lemon peel, finely chopped	1 oz
15 g	poppy seeds	½ oz
24	pecan nut halves	24
Lemon-vodka syrup		
175 g	clear honey	6 oz
4 tbsp	fresh lemon juice	4 tbsp
4 tbsp	vodka	4 tbsp

Crumble the fresh yeast into the milk, add 1 tablespoon of the sugar and stir well. Set the yeast solution aside until its surface becomes frothy — about 10 minutes; if using dried yeast, activate it according to the manufacturer's instructions. Stir 60 g (2 oz) of the flour into the yeast solution, and then leave the mixture in a warm place until it has doubled in bulk — about 30 minutes.

In a small bowl, beat the egg yolks with the remaining sugar, the vanilla and lemon rind. Dissolve the saffron in the vodka and add it to the egg mixture. In a separate bowl, whisk the egg whites with the salt until they are frothy and form soft peaks.

Sift the remaining flour and the semolina into a warm mixing bowl. Pour in the risen yeast and the egg yolk mixture then beat with a wooden spoon until a stiff mass is formed. Beat in two thirds of the egg whites, then fold in the remaining whites. Leave the dough to rest for 10 minutes, then knead it in the bowl for 10 minutes. Grease the surface of the dough lightly with a little of the melted butter, cover it with plastic film and set it aside in a warm place. When the dough has doubled in size — about 30 minutes — beat in the rest of the cooled melted butter, together with the candied peel and poppy seeds. Knead the dough for a few more minutes.

Lightly butter and flour twenty-four 7.5 cl (2½ fl oz) dariole moulds. Using a teaspoon, drop the dough into the moulds, filling them no more than a third full. Set the moulds aside in a warm place until the dough has more than doubled in size — 30 to 45 minutes. Meanwhile, preheat the oven to 190°C (375°F or Mark 5).

Bake the babas for 10 to 12 minutes, or until a skewer plunged to the base of the mould comes out clean. Unmould the babas immediately and cool them briefly on a wire rack.

To make the syrup, heat the honey and lemon juice in a non-reactive saucepan. When the mixture is hot, remove it from the heat and stir in the vodka. Trim the rounded, wider ends of the babas so they will sit flat on a plate. Pierce the babas in two or three places with a skewer, then pour a little of the hot syrup over each one. Serve the babas warm or cold, with half a pecan nut on top to decorate.

EDITOR'S NOTE: *For variety, the babas can be decorated with a little sifted icing sugar and served with thick Greek yogurt.*

Lime and Ginger Babas

Makes 10 babas
Working time: about 1 hour and 30 minutes
Total time: about 3 hours and 30 minutes (includes rising)

Per baba:
Calories **220**
Protein **8g**
Cholesterol **60mg**
Total fat **7g**
Saturated fat **4g**
Sodium **110mg**

15 g	fresh yeast, or ½ tsp dried yeast	½ oz
12.5 cl	skimmed milk, tepid	4 fl oz
1½ tbsp	light brown sugar	1½ tbsp
250 g	strong plain flour	8 oz
½ tsp	salt	½ tsp
2	eggs, beaten	2
60 g	unsalted butter, softened	2 oz
Lime and ginger syrup		
2 tbsp	light brown sugar	2 tbsp
1½ tbsp	fresh lime juice	1½ tbsp
4 tbsp	syrup from stem ginger jar	4 tbsp
1½ tbsp	brandy	1½ tbsp
Quark and grape filling		
250 g	quark	8 oz
2 tbsp	honey	2 tbsp
2 tsp	brandy	2 tsp
1 tsp	fresh lime juice	1 tsp
½ tsp	grated lime rind	½ tsp
1 tsp	pure vanilla extract	1 tsp
2	pieces preserved stem ginger (about 2.5 cm/1 inch each), finely chopped	2
15	black or green grapes, or a mixture of both, halved and pipped	15

Crumble the yeast into the milk, add 1 teaspoon of the sugar and mix well. Set the yeast solution aside until the surface becomes frothy — 10 to 15 minutes. If using dried yeast, activate it according to the manufacturer's instructions.

Sift the flour and salt into a warmed mixing bowl and form a hollow in the centre. Pour the yeast mixture and the eggs into the hollow and mix with a wooden spoon, gradually drawing in the flour. When all the ingredients are combined, steady the bowl with one hand and knead the dough with the other by lifting it up and slapping it back into the bowl for 7 to 10 minutes (the mixture will be too slack for conventional kneading). Spread the softened butter over the surface of the dough, then cover the bowl and set it aside in a warm place until it has tripled in bulk — about 1 hour.

Knock back the risen dough and add the remaining sugar. Use your hand to mix in the butter and sugar, then knead the dough again, as described above, for 2 minutes. Lightly butter and flour ten 10 cl (3½ fl oz) dariole moulds and half fill them with the dough. Set the moulds aside until the dough has risen to their tops — about 30 minutes. Meanwhile, preheat the oven to 190°C (375°F or Mark 5).

Bake the babas until they are brown and crisp on top and a skewer inserted into the centre comes out clean — about 15 minutes. Turn them out immediately, crisp side down, on to a wire rack.

To make the syrup, put the sugar in a small, non-reactive saucepan with 2 tablespoons of water and boil for 2 minutes. Add the lime juice and ginger syrup and return to the boil. Remove the pan from the heat and stir in the brandy. While the babas are still warm, pour the syrup into a shallow baking tin, large enough to contain all the babas in one layer. Add the babas, turning them quickly until all the syrup is absorbed.

For the filling, beat the quark in a bowl until smooth. Stir in the honey, brandy, lime juice, grated rind and vanilla extract, then fold in the chopped preserved ginger. With a sharp serrated knife, slice the babas in half lengthwise. Sandwich the halves back together with the filling and place them in foil or paper cases. Arrange the grape halves on top of the quark and chill slightly before serving.

Apple Streusel Tart

Serves 24
Working time: about 1 hour
Total time: about 3 hours (includes rising)

Calories **100**
Protein **2g**
Cholesterol **15mg**
Total fat **2g**
Saturated fat **1g**
Sodium **40mg**

10 g	fresh yeast, or ⅓ tsp dried yeast	⅓ oz
12.5 cl	skimmed milk, tepid	4 fl oz
45 g	light brown sugar	1½ oz
45 g	unsalted butter, melted	1½ oz
1	egg, beaten	1
250 g	strong plain flour	8 oz
½ tsp	salt	½ tsp
4	cardamom pods, husks removed and seeds ground	4
400 g	tart dessert apples	14 oz
2 tbsp	apricot jam	2 tbsp
Streusel topping		
60 g	plain flour	2 oz
1 tsp	ground cinnamon	1 tsp
30 g	light brown sugar	1 oz
30 g	unsalted butter, softened	1 oz

Crumble the yeast and dissolve it in one third of the milk with 1 teaspoon of the sugar. Leave the mixture in a warm place until its surface becomes frothy — 10 to 15 minutes; if using dried yeast, activate it according to the manufacturer's instructions. Meanwhile, dissolve the rest of the sugar in the remaining milk, then stir in the butter and the egg.

Sift the strong plain flour, salt and ground cardamom into a large, warmed mixing bowl. Form a well in the centre of the dry ingredients and pour in the yeast solution and the milk and egg mixture. Using a wooden spoon, blend the liquids together and gradually draw in the flour until all the ingredients are amalgamated. Continue to beat with the wooden spoon for 2 to 3 minutes, until the dough is smooth and slightly elastic (it will remain sticky). Cover the dough with plastic film and leave it in a warm place to rise for about 1 hour, until it has almost tripled in bulk.

Meanwhile, make the streusel topping. Combine the flour, cinnamon, brown sugar and softened butter in a mixing bowl and blend them together with your fingers until they form rough crumbs. Set the mixture aside. Preheat the oven to 180°C (350°F or Mark 4), and lightly butter a baking sheet.

Turn out the risen dough on to a floured board and knead it for 2 to 3 minutes, until smooth. Flatten the dough a little, dredge more flour over it and roll it out to form a 30 by 20 cm (12 by 8 inch) rectangle. Transfer the dough to the prepared baking sheet.

Core, halve and peel the apples, and slice them thinly. Arrange the slices in three parallel rows on top of the dough. Sprinkle the streusel topping around the edges and into the gaps between the rows. Bake the tart for 40 to 50 minutes, until the streusel is golden and the apples are soft.

While the tart is still warm, prepare a glaze. Mix the apricot jam with 2 tablespoons of water and bring it to the boil. Brush the apples with the glaze. Leave the tart to cool before serving.

Danish Pastries

Makes 26 pastries
Working time: about 1 hour and 10 minutes
Total time: about 3 hours and 15 minutes
(includes chilling and rising)

Per pastry:
Calories **75**
Protein **1g**
Cholesterol **10mg**
Total fat **4g**
Saturated fat **2g**
Sodium **20mg**

7 g	fresh yeast, or ¼ tsp dried yeast	¼ oz
250 g	strong plain flour	8 oz
¼ tsp	salt	¼ tsp
1 tsp	caster sugar	1 tsp
125 g	unsalted butter, chilled	4 oz
1	egg white	1
2 tbsp	apricot jam	2 tbsp
Fruit fillings		
2	fresh figs, peeled and chopped, or 2 dried figs, chopped	2
4	apricots, peeled, halved and stoned	4
2	nectarines or peaches, peeled, stoned and sliced	2

Blend the fresh yeast with 10 cl (3 fl oz) of warm water until dissolved; if using dried yeast, activate it according to the manufacturer's instructions. Sift the flour, salt and sugar into a bowl. Cut 30 g (1 oz) of the butter into small pieces and add it to the bowl; chill the remaining butter until required. With the fingertips, rub the butter into the flour until the mixture resembles fine

breadcrumbs. Add the yeast and egg white to the flour mixture and stir with a wooden spoon to make a soft dough. On a lightly floured surface, knead the dough for 10 minutes until smooth, elastic and no longer sticky. Place the dough in a polythene bag and chill it in the refrigerator for 30 minutes.

Roll out the dough to an oblong measuring about 50 by 20 cm (20 by 8 inches). Put the remaining butter between two sheets of greaseproof paper and roll it into a thin oblong about 30 by 15 cm (12 by 6 inches). Place the butter on the dough, covering about two thirds of its length. Fold the unbuttered third over half of the buttered dough; fold over the remaining buttered section. With a rolling pin or your hands, press down well on the dough to seal the edges.

Give the dough a quarter turn. Roll out the dough lightly, continuing to roll until it is an oblong about 50 by 20 cm (20 by 8 inches). Fold the dough into thirds again, wrap it in plastic film and refrigerate it for 20 minutes. Unwrap the dough, place it on a work surface with one of the short sides towards you and roll it into an oblong measuring 50 by 20 cm (20 by 8 inches). Fold the dough into thirds again, wrap it in film and refrigerate for 20 minutes. Repeat the turning, rolling, folding and refrigerating twice more.

Roll out the dough to an oblong measuring about 45 by 30 cm (18 by 12 inches). Cut the dough crosswise into three different-sized rectangles — 30 by 10 cm (12 by 4 inches), 30 by 15 cm (12 by 6 inches) and 30 by 20 cm (12 by 8 inches).

Spread the figs over the smallest rectangle, roll it up into a firm roll, then slice the roll into six pinwheels (opposite page, above). Place the pinwheels on a large baking sheet and cover them with a damp clean cloth or plastic film.

Cut the 30 by 15 cm (12 by 6 inch) rectangle into eight 7.5 cm (3 inch) squares. Place an apricot half in the centre of each square, make diagonal cuts from the corners to the edge of the apricot, and fold alternate points into the centre to form a windmill (opposite page, centre). Place on the baking sheet and cover.

Cut the remaining dough into six 10 cm (4 inch) squares, then cut each square in half diagonally, to form a total of 12 triangles. Place two nectarine slices on the longest edge of each triangle, roll up neatly and turn the ends in to make a crescent shape (opposite page, below). Place on the baking sheet with the other pastries and cover.

Leave the pastries for 40 to 50 minutes, until doubled in size. Meanwhile, preheat the oven to 250°C (450°F or Mark 8).

Bake the pastries for 10 to 15 minutes, until golden-brown and risen. While they are baking, heat the apricot jam until liquid in a small non-reactive saucepan, then pass it through a nylon sieve. Remove the pastries to a wire rack set over a tray; brush with the warm glaze and leave to cool for 15 to 20 minutes.

Making Pinwheels

1 *ROLLING UP THE DOUGH AND FILLING. Starting from one of the short ends, roll up the dough and fig filling as you would a Swiss roll. Keep the roll tight as you work, and ensure the ends of the roll remain aligned.*

2 *SLICING THE ROLL. Place the filled roll seam side down on a work surface. With a sharp knife, cut the roll into six equal slices.*

Shaping Windmills

1 *CUTTING DIAGONAL LINES. Place an apricot half in the centre of a 7.5 cm (3 inch) square of dough. With a sharp knife, cut a diagonal line from each corner to the edge of the apricot, so that you have four triangles joined in the middle.*

2 *FOLDING IN POINTS. Working in one direction, fold alternate points of the triangles into the centre, over the apricot. Press the final tip down firmly on top of the others, to make a secure join.*

Forming Crescents

1 *ENCLOSING THE FRUIT. Place two nectarine slices, one slightly overlapping another, along the longest side of a triangle of dough. Holding fruit and dough together, roll the base of the triangle towards the apex.*

2 *CURVING ROUND THE CRESCENT. Place the roll seam side down on the work surface. Gently shape both ends round to form a crescent.*

Raspberry Savarins

Makes 10 savarins
Working time: about 30 minutes
Total time: about 2 hours (includes rising)

Per savarin:
Calories **160**
Protein **3g**
Cholesterol **40mg**
Total fat **6g**
Saturated fat **3g**
Sodium **50mg**

7 g	*fresh yeast, or ¼ tsp dried yeast*	¼ oz
150 g	*plain flour*	5 oz
75 g	*caster sugar*	2½ oz
¼ tsp	*salt*	¼ tsp
1	*egg*	1
1	*egg white*	1
60 g	*unsalted butter, softened*	2 oz
1	*vanilla pod, or ¼ tsp pure vanilla extract*	1
4 tbsp	*eau-de-vie de framboise or kirsch*	4 tbsp
175 g	*fresh raspberries*	6 oz

Crumble the fresh yeast over 2 tablespoons of warm water and leave for about 5 minutes, or until the yeast has dissolved; if using dried yeast, activate it according to the manufacturer's instructions.

Sift the flour into a mixing bowl, blend in 15 g (½ oz) of the sugar and the salt, then make a well in the centre. Lightly beat the whole egg and egg white together and pour them into the well together with the yeast. Using a wooden spoon, beat the ingredients for 4 to 5 minutes, until they have formed a smooth, slightly elastic dough.

Cover the bowl with plastic film and put it in a warm place until the dough has risen to twice its original volume — about 30 minutes. Place the dough on a work surface and gradually work in the butter with your hands. Knead the dough briefly — 2 to 3 minutes — until smooth.

Preheat the oven to 200°C (400°F or Mark 6). Brush the insides of ten 7.5 cm (3 inch) dimple moulds or savarin moulds with melted butter. Divide the dough among them and leave in a warm place until it has risen to the top of the moulds — 20 to 30 minutes. Place the savarins on a baking sheet and bake them for about 15 minutes, until puffy and golden. Unmould them on to a wire rack set over a tray to cool.

In a small non-reactive saucepan, dissolve the remaining 60 g (2 oz) of sugar in 15 cl (¼ pint) of water and bring to the boil. Reduce the heat, then add the vanilla and simmer for 5 minutes. Allow to cool. Stir in the eau-de-vie or kirsch.

Spoon the syrup over the savarins, re-spooning any that drips on to the tray below. Fill the centres with the fresh raspberries and serve.

Miniature Kugelhopfs

A TRADITIONAL KUGELHOPF IS BAKED IN A FANCY FLUTED MOULD THAT HAS A CENTRAL FUNNEL TO ENSURE THE MIXTURE COOKS THROUGH EVENLY. FOR THESE SMALLER VERSIONS, THE FUNNEL IS UNNECESSARY.

Makes 12 kugelhopfs
Working time: about 1 hour
Total time: about 4 hours (includes rising)

Per kugelhopf:
Calories **165**
Protein **4g**
Cholesterol **50mg**
Total fat **5g**
Saturated fat **3g**
Sodium **20mg**

45 g	seedless raisins	1½ oz
15 g	fresh yeast, or ½ tsp dried yeast	½ oz
8 cl	skimmed milk, tepid	3 fl oz
275 g	strong plain flour	9 oz
⅛ tsp	salt	⅛ tsp
30 g	vanilla-flavoured caster sugar	1 oz
2	eggs, beaten	2
2 tbsp	dark rum (optional)	2 tbsp
60 g	unsalted butter, diced and softened	2 oz
30 g	candied mixed peel, chopped	1 oz
2 tsp	finely grated orange rind	2 tsp
2 tsp	finely grated lemon rind	2 tsp
	icing sugar, to decorate	

Put the raisins in a small bowl, pour boiling water over them and leave them to soak for at least 30 minutes. Crumble the fresh yeast into the milk and leave it in a warm place until it is frothy — 15 to 20 minutes; if using dried yeast, activate it according to the manufacturer's instructions.

Sift the flour and salt into a mixing bowl, stir in the vanilla sugar and form a well in the centre. Pour the eggs, rum (if you are using it) and yeast mixture into the well, then use a large wooden spoon or your hand to draw the ingredients together and form a smooth dough. Turn the dough on to a lightly floured surface and knead it well until it is firm and elastic — about 15 minutes. Gradually work the butter into the dough by first squeezing small pieces of butter between your fingers, then squeezing them into the dough. Continue until all the butter has been incorporated, then knead the dough briefly — 2 to 3 minutes. Transfer it to a very lightly oiled bowl, cover the bowl with plastic film and leave it in a warm place for 1½ to 2 hours, or until the dough has doubled in size.

Drain the raisins well, then mix them with the candied peel and the grated orange and lemon rind. Lightly butter twelve 6 to 7.5 cl (2 to 2½ fl oz) deep fluted moulds. Turn the dough on to a lightly floured work surface and work in the fruit mixture with your hands, spreading it evenly throughout the dough. Divide the dough into 12 equal portions and place one in each mould, pressing the dough well down. Cover the moulds with plastic film and leave them for about 30 minutes, or until the dough is well risen. Meanwhile, preheat the oven to 200°C (400°F or Mark 6).

Reduce the temperature to 190°C (375°F or Mark 5), then put the kugelhopfs into the oven and bake them for about 20 minutes, until the tops are browned and the sides have shrunk slightly from the moulds. Remove them from the oven and unmould them on to a wire rack to cool. Sift a little icing sugar over the surface of the kugelhopfs just before serving.

3 *Freshly baked brandy snaps, moulded while hot and pliable, harden into delicate horns as they cool (recipe, page 116).*

Delicate Confections

An exquisite selection of petits fours presented with after-dinner coffee can tempt even the most diet-conscious guest into indiscretion — so if they are to be served as part of a meal, it is best to substitute them for an ordinary dessert. Alternatively, they make the perfect accompaniment to morning coffee or afternoon tea. Petits fours are an ideal stand-by for unexpected visitors, since many can be stored for up to seven days, and most of them will keep for at least two or three days in an airtight container or in the refrigerator. Prettily boxed, they make an ideal gift.

Petits fours, literally, means "little ovens" — that is, little baked goods. In classic French patisserie these bite-sized sweetmeats are divided into two main categories — *rich* and *sec*. As their name suggests, traditional *petits fours riches* are sumptuous morsels, including such delights as tiny sponge shapes enrobed with fondant icing and decorated with sugar flowers and chocolate tracery. The iced sponge cakes on page 104 use a whisked fatless sponge and thinly applied glacé icing, but lack nothing in visual appeal or richness of taste.

Petits fours secs are more biscuit-like in appearance and texture; on the following pages you will find miniature versions of macaroons, brandy snaps and shortbread. Intermediate between these two categories are cakes such as the pistachio and almond petits fours on page 115, which contain relatively small amounts of sugar and will appeal to those who do not have a particularly sweet tooth.

Confectionery and fruit glazed with caramel also have a place among petits fours. In this section, the emphasis is on confections made with fruits and nuts, sparingly coated with fine caramel and chocolate.

Most of the recipes are simple. However, melting chocolate and making caramel require a little care and attention. When melting chocolate, choose a bowl that fits the saucepan exactly to prevent water from splashing into the chocolate; even one drop can turn the chocolate grainy. And never apply too much heat, since this causes white spots of cocoa butter to develop as the chocolate sets.

Before starting to make caramel, assemble all the ingredients and equipment, because once the syrup is ready you will have to apply it speedily before it starts to harden. To reduce the risk of the syrup crystallizing, ensure that every grain of sugar is dissolved before the syrup is brought to the boil, and stop stirring as soon as the syrup reaches the boil. Humidity prevents caramel from hardening and makes it sticky so, if possible, avoid making caramel on damp days or in a steamy kitchen.

Iced Sponge Cakes

Makes 30 cakes
Working time: about 1 hour and 25 minutes
Total time: about 1 hour and 40 minutes

Per cake:
Calories **95**
Protein **1g**
Cholesterol **25mg**
Total fat **3g**
Saturated fat **1g**
Sodium **10mg**

3	eggs	3
90 g	caster sugar	3 oz
90 g	plain flour	3 oz
2 tsp	strong black coffee, cooled	2 tsp
½ tsp	pure almond extract	½ tsp
1 tsp	cocoa powder, sifted	1 tsp
1 tbsp	desiccated coconut	1 tbsp

Icings and toppings		
100 g	plain chocolate, broken into pieces	3½ oz
3	crystallized violets, coarsely chopped	3
15 g	hazelnuts, toasted and skinned (page 29), chopped	½ oz
250 g	icing sugar	8 oz
15 g	unsalted butter, melted	½ oz
1 tsp	fresh lemon juice	1 tsp
½	orange, grated rind and 1 tsp juice only	½
2 tsp	strong black coffee, cooled	2 tsp
15 g	flaked almonds, toasted	½ oz
½	candied clementine, or other candied fruit, finely sliced	½
15 g	plain chocolate scrolls (page 12)	½ oz

Preheat the oven to 180°C (350°F or Mark 4). Lightly grease and flour 30 shallow tartlet tins of assorted shapes, each about 7.5 cm (3 inches) in diameter.

Place the eggs and caster sugar in a mixing bowl set over a pan of hot, but not boiling, water on a low heat. Using an electric hand-held mixer, whisk the eggs and sugar together until thick and pale. Remove the bowl from the heat and continue whisking until the mixture is cool and falls from the whisk in a ribbon trail. Sift the flour lightly over the surface of the mixture, then fold it in gently.

Divide the mixture equally among five small bowls. Leave one portion plain and flavour each of the others by stirring in one of the four flavourings: coffee, almond extract, cocoa powder and desiccated coconut. Spoon the mixtures evenly into the prepared tins and bake until they are golden — 10 to 15 minutes. Gently unmould them and leave to cool on a wire rack.

To ice the plain and coffee-flavoured cakes with chocolate icing, put the chocolate in a bowl with 6 tablespoons of water and place the bowl over a saucepan of simmering water until the chocolate melts, then stir. Let the chocolate cool and thicken slightly — about 5 minutes. Place one of the cakes on a metal spatula, hold it over the bowl and spoon the chocolate over it. Place the iced cake on a sheet of greaseproof paper. Ice the remaining plain and coffee-flavoured cakes in the same way. Decorate each plain cake with a piece of crystallized violet and sprinkle chopped hazelnuts over the coffee-flavoured cakes, then leave the cakes to set.

To ice the remaining cakes, mix the icing sugar with the butter and 3 tablespoons of warm water. Divide this into three portions: flavour one with the lemon juice, one with the grated orange rind and orange juice, and the third with the coffee. Using the same technique as for the chocolate icing, cover the almond cakes with lemon icing, the coconut cakes with orange icing, and the chocolate cakes with coffee icing. Decorate them with the flaked almonds, candied clementines and chocolate scrolls respectively.

EDITOR'S NOTE: *To toast flaked almonds, put them under the grill for about 2 minutes until golden, shaking them constantly.*

Fruited Turkish Coffee Squares.

Makes 70 squares
Working time: about 30 minutes
Total time: about 1 hour and 30 minutes

Per square:
Calories **35**
Protein **1g**
Cholesterol **5mg**
Total fat **1g**
Saturated fat **0g**
Sodium **25mg**

250 g	plain flour	8 oz
1 tsp	ground cinnamon	1 tsp
½ tsp	ground coriander	½ tsp
1 tbsp	coffee beans, very finely ground	1 tbsp
100 g	muscovado sugar	3½ oz
100 g	polyunsaturated margarine	3½ oz
1	egg, beaten	1
2	large bananas, peeled and very thinly sliced lengthwise	2
175 g	fresh apricots, stoned and very thinly sliced	6 oz
½ tsp	bicarbonate of soda	½ tsp
½ tsp	baking powder	½ tsp
¼ litre	plain low-fat yogurt	8 fl oz
1 tbsp	icing sugar	1 tbsp

Preheat the oven to 200°C (400°F or Mark 6).

Sift the flour, cinnamon, coriander and coffee together in a mixing bowl. Add the muscovado sugar and rub in the margarine until fine crumbs are formed. Divide the mixture into two portions in separate bowls. Add half the beaten egg to one portion, and mix with your hands to give larger crumbs and a slightly sticky consistency. Press this mixture firmly into the base of a tin measuring about 25 by 18 cm (10 by 7 inches) and at least 4 cm (1½ inches) deep. Arrange the banana slices in rows over the crumb base, and lay rows of apricot slices on top.

Stir the bicarbonate of soda into the remaining fine crumb mixture; blend the baking powder with the remaining egg and add this and the yogurt to the crumbs. Mix well with a wooden spoon until smooth, then pour over the fruit in the tin, ensuring that the fruit is completely covered. Bake in the oven until firm to the touch — 30 to 40 minutes. Remove from the oven and leave to cool in the tin.

When cool, sift the icing sugar over the top and cut into 2.5 cm (1 inch) squares to serve.

EDITOR'S NOTE: *To give the squares a crunchier top, omit the icing sugar and sprinkle a tablespoon of demerara sugar over the mixture before it is baked in the oven. The squares may be stored in the refrigerator for two days.*

Candied Fruit Cake Squares

Makes 64 squares
Working time: about 1 hour
Total time: about 5 hours and 30 minutes (includes drying)

Per square:			
Calories **50**	1	large thick-skinned grapefruit, peel only	1
Protein **trace**	175 g	light brown sugar	6 oz
Cholesterol **10mg**	125 g	stoned dates, cut into 1 cm (½ inch) pieces	4 oz
Total fat **1g**			
Saturated fat **trace**	100 g	red glacé cherries, halved	3½ oz
Sodium **15mg**	60 g	candied green figs or angelica, cut into strips	2 oz
	100 g	shelled walnuts, roughly chopped	3½ oz
	125 g	raisins	4 oz
	3	eggs, beaten	3
	125 g	muscovado sugar	4 oz
	1 tsp	pure vanilla extract	1 tsp
	1	lemon, grated rind only	1
	100 g	plain flour	3½ oz
	1 tsp	baking powder	1 tsp
	1 tsp	ground cinnamon	1 tsp
	½ tsp	ground mixed spice	½ tsp
	3 tbsp	brandy or whisky	3 tbsp
	175 g	apricot jam	6 oz

Place the grapefruit peel in a saucepan, cover with cold water and bring slowly to the boil, then drain thoroughly. Repeat this process three more times to rid the peel of excess bitterness. Cover the peel with cold water once more, bring to the boil and simmer gently until the peel is soft but not breaking up — 20 to 30 minutes. Drain the peel, reserving the water.

Prepare a syrup in a saucepan by dissolving the light brown sugar in 12.5 cl (4 fl oz) of the reserved water over a gentle heat. Add the peel and cook it gently, uncovered, for another 20 to 30 minutes, until it is completely translucent. Remove the peel from the pan and leave it on a wire rack for a few hours, until it is dry to the touch and easy to handle (or dry it for an hour in the oven at its lowest setting).

Preheat the oven to 170°C (325°F or Mark 3). Cut the dried peel into 1 cm (½ inch) pieces and place them in a large mixing bowl. Mix in the dates, cherries, figs, walnuts and raisins. In another bowl, blend the beaten eggs with the muscovado sugar, vanilla and lemon rind. Sift the flour with the baking powder, cinnamon and mixed spice into the bowl with the beaten eggs, and blend to a batter. Pour this mixture on to the fruit and stir well, ensuring that each piece of fruit is lightly covered with batter.

Line a shallow 25 cm (10 inch) square baking tin with non-stick parchment paper. Pour the mixture into the lined tin, level the surface and bake in the oven for about 1 hour, or until set. Remove the cake from the oven, prick the surface all over with a fork and dribble on the brandy. Leave to cool in the tin for 15 minutes before transferring to a wire rack to cool completely.

Cut the cake into 3 cm (1¼ inch) squares. Heat the jam gently until it is liquid, then press it through a nylon sieve. Brush the glaze over and around each square.

EDITOR'S NOTE: *Closely wrapped in foil, the cake may be left to mature for two days before it is cut into squares — this will give a moister result. If you are serving the cake without forks, brush the tops of the squares only with just 60 g (2 oz) of glaze to make them less sticky to handle. The squares will keep for about four weeks in an airtight container.*

Chocolate Kisses

Makes 36 kisses
Working time: about 40 minutes
Total time: about 50 minutes

Per kiss:
Calories **65**
Protein **1g**
Cholesterol **0mg**
Total fat **2g**
Saturated fat **1g**
Sodium **5mg**

60 g	plain chocolate, broken into pieces	2 oz
125 g	blanched almonds, toasted and finely ground	4 oz
125 g	shelled hazelnuts, toasted and skinned (page 29), finely ground	4 oz
90 g	cornmeal	3 oz
90 g	icing sugar	3 oz
90 g	caster sugar	3 oz
1 tbsp	clear honey	1 tbsp
2	egg whites	2
5 tbsp	apricot jam without added sugar	5 tbsp

Preheat the oven to 220°C (425°F or Mark 7). Line two large baking sheets with non-stick parchment paper.

Melt the chocolate in a heatproof bowl set over a pan of simmering water. Place the almonds, hazelnuts, cornmeal, icing sugar, caster sugar and honey in a mixing bowl. Pour on the melted chocolate and stir the mixture thoroughly, then add the egg whites and stir again until a stiff batter is formed.

Spoon the mixture into a piping bag fitted with a 5 mm (¼ inch) star nozzle. Pipe 72 rosettes, each about 4 cm (1½ inches) in diameter, at least 2.5 cm (1 inch) apart, on to the prepared baking sheets.

Bake the rosettes until they are set — 8 to 10 minutes — then transfer them to wire racks and leave them to cool. Just before serving, sandwich the rosettes together in pairs, using the jam as filling.

EDITOR'S NOTE: *To toast almonds, put them on a baking sheet under a hot grill for 2 to 3 minutes, or until golden; turn or shake them constantly.*

Glacé Fruit Diamonds

THIS RECIPE IS REMINISCENT OF THE FAMOUS FLORENTINE
SPECIALITY, BUT OMITS THE TRADITIONAL CHOCOLATE COATING
AND USES GREEK YOGURT INSTEAD OF DOUBLE CREAM
IN THE MIXTURE.

Makes about 30 diamonds
Working time: about 25 minutes
Total time: about 45 minutes

Per diamond:
Calories **70**
Protein **1g**
Cholesterol **5mg**
Total fat **4g**
Saturated fat **1g**
Sodium **10mg**

45 g	unsalted butter	1 ½ oz
125 g	thick Greek yogurt	4 oz
90 g	light brown sugar	3 oz
125 g	blanched almonds, 90 g (3 oz) chopped, the remainder slivered	4 oz
60 g	glacé cherries, quartered	2 oz
45 g	glacé clementines, chopped	1 ½ oz
45 g	glacé figs, chopped	1 ½ oz
45 g	glacé plums, chopped	1 ½ oz
30 g	crystallized orange peel, finely chopped	1 oz
60 g	plain flour, sifted	2 oz

Preheat the oven to 180°C (350°F or Mark 4). Line the base of a 32 by 22 cm (13 by 9 inch) Swiss roll tin with non-stick parchment paper.

Gently heat the butter, yogurt and sugar in a saucepan until the butter melts and the sugar dissolves. Remove the pan from the heat and stir in the almonds, glacé fruit, crystallized orange peel and flour. Using a metal spatula, spread the mixture evenly in the prepared tin and bake it until it is golden-brown and firm to the touch — 20 to 25 minutes.

Let the mixture cool a little in the tin, then transfer it to a cutting board. Peel off the parchment paper and cut into small diamonds for serving.

EDITOR'S NOTE: *A different selection of glacé fruits can be used in place of those listed above.*

Almond Petits Fours with Kumquat and Ginger

Makes: 30 petits fours
Working time: about 30 minutes
Total time: about 50 minutes

Per petit four:	125 g	caster sugar, plus 2 teaspoons for the glaze	4 oz
Calories **60**	2	egg whites, lightly beaten	2
Protein **1g**	175 g	ground almonds	6 oz
Cholesterol **0mg**	1	orange, finely grated rind and juice	1
Total fat **4g**	¼ tsp	pure vanilla extract	¼ tsp
Saturated fat **1g**	5	kumquats, sliced and seeded	5
Sodium **5mg**	2 tsp	diced preserved stem ginger	2 tsp

Preheat the oven to 180°C (350°F or Mark 4). Line a baking sheet with non-stick parchment paper.

In a mixing bowl, combine the 125 g (4 oz) of caster sugar with the egg whites, ground almonds, orange rind and vanilla extract to form a soft paste. Transfer the mixture to a piping bag fitted with a 2 cm (¾ inch) star nozzle and pipe 30 small rosettes on to the parchment paper. Decorate the top of each rosette with one slice of kumquat and a little diced ginger. Bake the petits fours in the oven until they are golden-brown — about 20 minutes.

Meanwhile, prepare the glaze. Put the orange juice and the remaining sugar in a small saucepan. Heat gently, stirring until the sugar has dissolved, then increase the heat and boil the mixture rapidly for 3 to 4 minutes until it becomes syrupy.

While the petits fours are still warm, paint the orange glaze over the kumquat and ginger. Allow to cool before serving.

Chocolate-Tipped Horseshoes

Makes 30 horseshoes
Working time: about 30 minutes
Total time: about 1 hour

Per horseshoe:			
Calories **100**	125 g	unsalted butter	4 oz
Protein **1g**	100 g	icing sugar, sifted	3½ oz
Cholesterol **25mg**	2	egg yolks	2
Total fat **5g**	1 tsp	pure vanilla extract	1 tsp
Saturated fat **3g**	175 g	plain flour	6 oz
Sodium **75mg**	90 g	cornmeal	3 oz
	45 g	plain chocolate, broken into pieces	1½ oz
	45 g	white chocolate, broken into pieces	1½ oz

Preheat the oven to 170°C (325°F or Mark 3). Line two large baking sheets with non-stick parchment paper.

Beat the butter and sugar together in a mixing bowl until light and fluffy. Beat in the egg yolks and vanilla extract, sift in the flour and cornmeal, and continue to beat until the ingredients are thoroughly combined.

Take a piece of the dough and roll it between the palms of your hands into a rope about 1 cm (½ inch) thick. Cut the rope into 10 cm (4 inch) lengths, then curve each piece into a horseshoe shape and place it on the baking parchment. Roll and shape the remaining dough in the same way, spacing the horseshoes well apart on the parchment to allow for spreading. There should be 30 horseshoes in all.

Bake the horseshoes until they are lightly browned — 15 to 20 minutes — then transfer them to wire racks and let them cool.

Melt the plain and white chocolate in separate heat-proof bowls set over pans of simmering water. Dip the ends of half of the horseshoes in the plain chocolate and the remaining horseshoes in the white chocolate. Place them on a tray lined with non-stick parchment paper and let the chocolate set before serving.

Ganache-Filled Macaroons

CLASSIC CHOCOLATE GANACHE IS A LIGHT WHISKED MIXTURE
OF MELTED CHOCOLATE AND DOUBLE CREAM. THIS LOW-FAT
VERSION USES YOGURT INSTEAD OF CREAM AND
NEEDS NO WHISKING.

Makes 16 macaroons
Working time: about 30 minutes
Total time: about 1 hour and 15 minutes

Per macaroon:
Calories **80**
Protein **2g**
Cholesterol **0mg**
Total fat **4g**
Saturated fat **1g**
Sodium **10mg**

25 g	ground almonds	4 oz
90 g	caster sugar	3 oz
2	egg whites	2
½ tsp	pure almond extract	½ tsp
30 g	plain chocolate	1 oz
1 tbsp	thick Greek yogurt	1 tbsp
1 tsp	icing sugar	1 tsp

Preheat the oven to 180°C (350°F or Mark 4). Line one large or two small baking sheets with non-stick parchment paper.

Put the almonds and caster sugar into a mixing bowl and mix well together. In a small bowl, lightly whisk one egg white with the almond extract until frothy, then pour them into the almond mixture. Mix well together to form a soft paste. Spoon the paste into a piping bag fitted with 1.5 cm (⅝ inch) plain nozzle. Pipe 32 small 2.5 cm (1 inch) mounds of the almond mixture on to the lined baking sheet, spacing them 1 cm (½ inch)

apart. Put the remaining egg white into a small bowl and whisk it lightly with a fork, just enough to break it up. Brush each of the mounds of almond mixture with egg white, flattening any points as you do so.

Bake the macaroons for 10 to 15 minutes, until they are lightly browned. Remove them from the oven and allow them to cool on the baking sheet for a minute or two, then remove them from the parchment paper and, using a finger, press in the flat side of each macaroon to make a small indentation. Place the macaroons on a wire rack to cool.

To make the ganache, melt the chocolate in a heat-proof bowl over a saucepan of simmering water. Remove the bowl from the heat and stir in the yogurt. Refrigerate for 5 to 10 minutes, until the ganache begins to thicken.

Sandwich pairs of macaroons together with the ganache and replace them on the wire rack. Leave in a cool place for about 5 minutes until the filling sets firmly. Lightly sift icing sugar over the macaroons and place them in small petits fours cases to serve.

EDITOR'S NOTE: *The filled macaroons will keep for five to six days stored in an airtight container.*

Fig and Orange Petits Fours

Makes 28 petits fours
Working time: about 40 minutes
Total time: about 1 hour

Per petit four:
Calories **45**
Protein **trace**
Cholesterol **trace**
Total fat **3g**
Saturated fat **1g**
Sodium **10mg**

30 g	unsalted butter	1 oz
30 g	polyunsaturated margarine	1 oz
1	orange, finely grated rind only	1
30 g	clear honey	1 oz
1	egg white	1
60 g	ground almonds	2 oz
30 g	cornflour, sifted	1 oz
30 g	plain flour, sifted	1 oz
30 g	stoned dates, chopped	1 oz
60 g	dried figs, chopped	2 oz
30 g	candied orange peel, chopped	1 oz
	icing sugar (optional)	
	glacé fruits, dried fruits and candied orange peel (optional)	
	shelled pistachio nuts, skinned and chopped (optional)	

Preheat the oven to 190°C (375°F or Mark 5). Very lightly butter 28 petits fours moulds, each approximately 4 cm (1½ inches) across.

Put the butter, margarine, orange rind and honey into a mixing bowl and beat well together until light and fluffy. Gradually beat in the egg white, then fold in the ground almonds, cornflour, plain flour, chopped dates, figs and candied peel.

Fill the prepared moulds with the creamed mixture and level the tops with a round-bladed knife. Place the moulds on a baking sheet. Bake for 5 to 10 minutes until risen, lightly browned and firm to the touch. Carefully unmould on to a wire rack to cool.

Serve in petits fours cases, either plain or — as shown here — decorated with a little sifted icing sugar, glacé and dried fruits, candied peel or chopped nuts as desired.

EDITOR'S NOTE: *To skin pistachio nuts, drop them into boiling water and simmer for 1 minute. Drain thoroughly, then wrap them in a towel and rub them vigorously until they have shed their skins.*

Apricot and Hazelnut Petits Fours

THIS RECIPE IS IDEAL FOR USING UP GENOESE SPONGE
TRIMMINGS THAT MAY BE LEFT OVER FROM SEVERAL
OF THE RECIPES IN CHAPTER 2.

Makes 24 petits fours
Working time: about 20 minutes
Total time: about 1 hour and 20 minutes (includes chilling)

Per petit four:
Calories **35**
Protein **1g**
Cholesterol **10mg**
Total fat **2g**
Saturated fat **0g**
Sodium **20mg**

125 g	genoese sponge (recipe, page 11), or other plain sponge cake	4 oz
60 g	dried apricots, finely chopped	2 oz
30 g	shelled hazelnuts, toasted and skinned (page 29), finely chopped or coarsely ground	1 oz
2 tbsp	orange-flavoured liqueur	2 tbsp
2 tbsp	apricot jam without added sugar	2 tbsp
2 tsp	icing sugar	2 tsp

Place the sponge cake in a food processor or blender and process it into crumbs; alternatively, rub the sponge cake through a wire sieve. Put the crumbs into a mixing bowl with the chopped apricots, hazelnuts, orange-flavoured liqueur and apricot jam, and mix them well together.

Gather up the mixture in your hands and roll it out, using your palms, into a long, thin roll. Flatten the top and sides of the roll a little, then cut it into 24 equal slices. Lay the slices flat on the work surface and sift the icing sugar over them.

Place each slice in a petit four case. Chill the petits fours for at least 1 hour before serving.

Chocolate-Apricot Petits Fours

Makes 40 petits fours
Working time: about 1 hour
Total time: about 2 hours (includes chilling)

Per petit four:
Calories **70**
Protein **1g**
Cholesterol **15mg**
Total fat **4g**
Saturated fat **2g**
Sodium **5mg**

150 g	plain flour	5 oz
30 g	icing sugar	1 oz
90 g	unsalted butter, diced	3 oz
2	egg yolks	2
125 g	ground almonds	4 oz
60 g	caster sugar	2 oz
90 g	ready-to-eat dried apricots, finely chopped	3 oz
1 tbsp	apricot-flavoured liqueur	1 tbsp
½	lightly whisked egg white	½
2 tbsp	apricot jam	2 tbsp
45 g	plain chocolate, broken into pieces	1½ oz

Sift the flour and icing sugar into a mixing bowl, then rub in the butter until the mixture resembles fine breadcrumbs. Add the egg yolks and mix together with a round-bladed knife to make a fairly stiff dough. Knead the dough very lightly until smooth then wrap it in plastic film and refrigerate for 30 minutes. Lightly grease one large or two small baking sheets.

Roll out the chilled dough, on a lightly floured surface, to a thickness of 3 mm (⅛ inch). Prick the dough well all over with a fork. Using a 5.5 cm (2¼ inch) fluted cutter, stamp out rounds from the dough and place them on the prepared baking sheet. Re-knead and re-

roll the trimmings, prick the dough again, then stamp out more rounds. Continue until all the dough is used up — you should have about 40 rounds. Refrigerate the rounds for 30 minutes. Meanwhile, preheat the oven to 190°C (375°F or Mark 5).

Bake the rounds for 10 to 12 minutes until they are lightly browned. Remove the biscuits from the baking sheet to a wire rack to cool.

Put the ground almonds, caster sugar and chopped apricots into a bowl and mix well together. Mix in the apricot liqueur and just sufficient egg white to make a stiff paste. On a surface very lightly sifted with icing sugar, knead the apricot paste until smooth, then roll it out about 3 mm (⅛ inch) thick. Using a 4.5 cm (1¾ inch) plain cutter, stamp out rounds from the apricot paste. Re-knead and re-roll the trimmings and cut out more rounds, again continuing until all the paste is used up and you have about 40 rounds.

Heat the jam in a small pan until boiling, pass it through a nylon sieve, then brush each biscuit base lightly with the glaze. Place a round of apricot paste on each biscuit, pressing it firmly in position. Lay the petits fours out in a single layer on wire racks.

Melt the chocolate in a small heatproof bowl over a pan of simmering water. Fold a greaseproof paper piping bag *(page 13)*, and fill it with the melted chocolate. Fold the top of the bag down and cut off the tip. Decorate each petit four with fine chocolate piping *(page 13)*. Leave them in a cool place for 10 to 15 minutes to set.

EDITOR'S NOTE: *The petits fours may be stored in an airtight container for three to four days.*

Pistachio and Almond Petits Fours

THESE PETITS FOURS MAKE A DELIGHTFUL AFTER-DINNER TREAT SERVED WITH COFFEE.

Makes 28 petits fours
Working time: about 30 minutes
Total time: about 45 minutes

Per petit four:
Calories **60**
Protein **1g**
Cholesterol **10mg**
Total fat **4g**
Saturated fat **1g**
Sodium **15mg**

125 g	ground almonds	4 oz
90 g	caster sugar	3 oz
30 g	cornflour	1 oz
30 g	polyunsaturated margarine, melted and cooled	1 oz
1 tbsp	soured cream	1 tbsp
1	egg, beaten	1
1 tbsp	kirsch or amaretto liqueur	1 tbsp
30 g	shelled pistachio nuts, skinned and chopped	1 oz
1 tbsp	icing sugar	1 tbsp

Preheat the oven to 190°C (375°F or Mark 5). Have ready 28 double-thickness petits fours cases.

Mix together the almonds, caster sugar and corn-flour in a mixing bowl. Make a well in the centre then pour in the margarine, soured cream, egg and kirsch or amaretto. Using a wooden spoon, blend the ingredients together until smooth.

Spoon the almond mixture into the petits fours cases, filling each one three-quarters full. Sprinkle the pistachio nuts evenly over the top of the mixture, then sift on the icing sugar.

Place the petits fours on a baking sheet and bake for 12 to 15 minutes, until risen, very lightly browned and firm to the touch. Remove from the baking sheet to a wire rack to cool.

EDITOR'S NOTE: *These petits fours are best eaten on the day they are made, but they may be kept for two to three days stored in an airtight container. To skin pistachio nuts, drop them into boiling water and simmer for 1 minute, drain thoroughly, then rub them briskly in a towel.*

Ginger Snaps with Kumquat and Ginger Mousse

Makes about 20 ginger snaps
Working time: about 1 hour and 15 minutes
Total time: about 2 hours and 30 minutes

Per snap:
Calories **75**
Protein **2g**
Cholesterol **10mg**
Total fat **4g**
Saturated fat **2g**
Sodium **15mg**

60 g	unsalted butter	2 oz
60 g	light brown sugar	2 oz
2 tbsp	golden syrup	2 tbsp
60 g	plain flour, sifted	2 oz
1 tsp	fresh lemon juice	1 tsp
½ tsp	ground ginger	½ tsp
Kumquat and ginger mousse		
175 g	kumquats, stalked	6 oz
6 tbsp	fresh orange juice	6 tbsp
1 ½ tsp	powdered gelatine	1 ½ tsp
2.5 cm	piece stem ginger	1 inch
2 tsp	syrup from stem ginger jar	2 tsp
250 g	fromage frais	8 oz

First, make the mousse. Purée the kumquats in a food processor or blender with 4 tablespoons of the orange juice. Pass the purée through a fine sieve, and discard the pips. Put the remaining orange juice into a small bowl, sprinkle on the gelatine and allow it to soften for 2 minutes. Place the bowl over a pan of simmering water and stir until the gelatine has dissolved.

Return the kumquat purée to the processor and add the stem ginger, ginger syrup and *fromage frais.* Process until smooth. Add the gelatine and process for another 20 seconds. Transfer the mixture to a bowl and refrigerator until set — about 1½ hours.

Preheat the oven to 180°C (350°F or Mark 4). Grease two baking sheets, and line them with non-stick parchment paper. Gently heat the butter, sugar and golden syrup in a small, heavy-bottomed saucepan. When the butter has melted and the sugar has dissolved, remove the saucepan from the heat and stir in the flour. Mix well until smooth and then stir in the lemon juice and ground ginger.

Drop 4 level teaspoons of the mixture on to each baking sheet, spacing them well apart. Put one sheet in the oven and bake until the snaps are bubbly and golden-brown — about 10 minutes. Half way through the cooking time, put the other sheet in the oven. When the snaps on the first sheet are done, remove them from the oven and let them stand for about 1 minute, to firm up slightly. Lift the snaps from the parchment with a metal spatula and shape them into cornets round a metal cream horn mould *(opposite page).* Place the shaped snaps on a wire rack.

Wipe the parchment with paper towels, refill the sheet with 4 more level teaspoons of mixture and return it to the oven. Remove the second sheet of cooked snaps from the oven. Let them rest briefly, then shape them as before. Continue to cook and shape the snaps in batches of four, until all the mixture has been used up. If the snaps start to harden before they are shaped, return them to the oven for a few seconds to soften them again.

Just before serving, transfer the mousse to a piping bag fitted with a 1 cm (½ inch) plain nozzle and fill the snaps. The snaps will hold the mixture for about an hour without becoming soft.

Chocolate Brandy Snaps

Makes 20 snaps
Working and (total time): about 1 hour and 15 minutes

Per snap:
Calories **60**
Protein **1g**
Cholesterol **5mg**
Total fat **5g**
Saturated fat **3g**
Sodium **5mg**

60 g	unsalted butter	2 oz
60 g	light brown sugar	2 oz
2 tbsp	golden syrup	2 tbsp
60 g	plain flour, sifted	2 oz
1 tsp	fresh lemon juice	1 tsp
½ tsp	ground cinnamon	½ tsp
150 g	plain chocolate, broken into pieces	5 oz

Preheat the oven to 180°C (350°F or Mark 4). Grease two baking sheets and line them with non-stick parchment paper.

Put the butter, sugar and golden syrup in a small saucepan and stir them over a low heat. When the butter has melted and the sugar dissolved, remove the pan from the heat and stir in the flour. Mix until smooth, then stir in the lemon juice and cinnamon.

Drop 4 level teaspoons of the mixture on to each baking sheet, spacing them well apart. Put one sheet in the oven and bake the snaps until they are bubbly and golden-brown — about 10 minutes. Half way through the cooking time, put the other sheet in the oven. When the snaps on the first sheet are done, remove them from the oven and let them stand for a minute or so, to firm up slightly. Carefully lift them off the baking sheet with a metal spatula and roll them into cylinders round the handle of a wooden spoon, as shown below. Place the shaped snaps on a wire rack.

Wipe the parchment with paper towels, refill the sheet with 4 more teaspoons of mixture and return it to the oven. Remove the second sheet of cooked snaps from the oven. Let them rest briefly, then shape them as before. Cook and shape the remaining mixture in batches in the same way. If the snaps start to harden before they are shaped, return them to the oven for a few seconds to soften them again.

When all the snaps are cooked and cool, melt the chocolate in a heatproof bowl set over a saucepan of hot water. Dip the ends of the snaps in the chocolate, and leave them to set on non-stick parchment paper.

EDITOR'S NOTE: *The brandy snaps can be stored for up to a week in an airtight container.*

Shaping Brandy Snaps

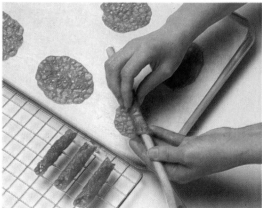

ROLLING CYLINDERS. Remove the snaps from the oven and leave them just long enough to be lifted without tearing — about 1 minute. Lift one snap from the sheet with a metal spatula and quickly roll it round the handle of a wooden spoon. Slide the cylinder off the spoon handle as soon as it has set and place it on a wire rack. Shape the remaining snaps in the same way.

MOULDING CORNETS. Remove the snaps from the oven and leave them just long enough to be lifted without tearing — about 1 minute. Lift one snap from the sheet with a metal spatula and press it round a metal cream horn mould to shape it into a cornet. Transfer the cornet to a wire rack as soon as it has set in shape. Shape the remaining snaps in the same way.

Tulip Snaps with Amaretto Mousse

Makes 10 snaps
Working time: about 45 minutes
Total time: about 1 hour and 30 minutes (includes chilling)

Per snap:
Calories **110**
Protein **2g**
Cholesterol **10mg**
Total fat **7g**
Saturated fat **3g**
Sodium **10mg**

30 g	unsalted butter	1 oz
30 g	light brown sugar	1 oz
1 tbsp	golden syrup	1 tbsp
30 g	plain flour, sifted	1 oz
½ tsp	fresh lemon juice	½ tsp
½ tsp	ground cinnamon	½ tsp
5	blanched almonds, split and toasted	5
Amaretto mousse		
2 tsp	powdered gelatine	2 tsp
250 g	fromage frais	8 oz
60 g	amaretti biscuits, crushed to a fine powder	2 oz
1 tbsp	amaretto liqueur	1 tbsp

First make the mousse. Sprinkle the gelatine over 3 tablespoons of water in a small bowl. Leave it to soften for 2 minutes, then place the bowl over a saucepan of simmering water and stir until the gelatine has completely dissolved. In a separate bowl, mix together the *fromage frais*, crushed amaretti biscuits and amaretto liqueur. Add the gelatine and stir the mixture thoroughly. Chill the mousse in the refrigerator until it has set — about 1 hour.

Meanwhile, make the tulip snaps. Preheat the oven to 180°C (350°F or Mark 4). Grease two baking sheets and line them with non-stick parchment paper.

Put the butter, sugar and golden syrup into a small saucepan over a low heat and stir until the butter has melted and the sugar dissolved. Remove the pan from the heat and stir in the flour. Mix until smooth, then stir in the lemon juice and cinnamon. Drop 4 level teaspoons of the mixture, spaced well apart, on to each of the baking sheets. Put one sheet in the oven and bake the snaps until they are bubbly and golden-brown — about 10 minutes. Half way through the cooking time, put the other sheet in the oven.

When the snaps on the first sheet are done, remove them from the oven and let them stand for a minute or so, to firm up slightly. Lift the snaps off the baking sheet with a metal spatula and drape them, topside down, over the bases of four upturned narrow glasses. The snaps will set in a tulip shape. Wipe the parchment with paper towels, refill the sheet with the last 2 teaspoons of mixture and return it to the oven. Remove the second sheet of cooked snaps from the oven. Let them rest briefly while you transfer the first batch to a wire rack, then shape them in the same way. Finally, shape the remaining two snaps.

When the tulip snaps are firm, spoon the mousse into a piping bag fitted with a 1 cm (½ inch) star nozzle and pipe a rosette of the mixture into each tulip. Decorate the mousse with a half almond.

EDITOR'S NOTE: *To toast split almonds, put them under a hot grill for 2 to 3 minutes, or until golden; turn or shake them constantly.*

Nut-Filled Fruits

Makes 36 fruits
Working (and total) time: about 1 hour

Per fruit:			
Calories **30**	12	fresh dates	12
Protein **1g**	12	small ready-to-eat dried apricots	12
Cholesterol **0mg**	6	large ready-to-eat stoned prunes	6
Total fat **1g**	18	shelled pistachio nuts, skinned and halved	18
Saturated fat **trace**			
Sodium **5mg**	1 tsp	icing sugar	1 tsp
	175 g	granulated sugar	6 oz
	Nut filling		
	30 g	shelled pistachio nuts, skinned and finely ground	1 oz
	30 g	ground almonds	1 oz
	30 g	icing sugar	1 oz
	½	lightly whisked egg white	½

First make the filling. Put the ground pistachio nuts, ground almonds and icing sugar into a mixing bowl and mix well together with a wooden spoon, then add just sufficient egg white to bind the mixture into a stiff paste. Knead very lightly until smooth.

Very carefully slit each date lengthwise and remove the stone — do not cut the dates completely in half. Slit each apricot in half lengthwise — again, do not cut the fruit completely in half. Cut each prune in half lengthwise, then smooth out each half prune to make a neat cup shape.

Divide the nut paste into 36 small pieces, and shape each piece into a neat oval shape by rolling it between your fingers. Fill the dates, apricots and prune halves with the tiny ovals of nut paste, closing the fruits neatly round the sides of the filling. Decorate six of each type of filled fruit with a pistachio half, sift the icing sugar over them, place in petits fours cases and set aside.

Next, prepare a pan of caramel. Very lightly butter a baking sheet. Put the granulated sugar into a small heavy-bottomed saucepan with 3 tablespoons of cold water. Stir over a low heat until every crystal of sugar has dissolved, brushing down any that stick to the sides of the pan with a bristle pastry brush dipped in hot water. When the sugar has completely dissolved, bring the syrup to the boil and boil it gently until it just turns to a very pale caramel colour, or until the temperature on a sugar thermometer registers between 160° and 170°C (320° and 338°F). Immediately, plunge the base of the saucepan into cold water to arrest the cooking and prevent the caramel darkening any further. Then, to keep the caramel fluid, stand the pan in a bowl of very hot water.

Working very quickly, balance the remaining fruits, one at a time, on the end of a fork and dip them in the caramel. Allow the excess caramel to run back into the pan. Place the dipped fruits on the buttered baking sheet and decorate each one with a pistachio half; if the caramel begins to thicken, carefully re-heat it.

Leave the dipped fruits in a cool place for 5 to 10 minutes until the caramel has set hard. Remove the fruits from the baking sheet and place them in petits fours cases. Arrange them, together with the sugar-coated fruits, on a serving dish.

EDITOR'S NOTE: *The caramel-dipped fruits may be stored in an airtight container, in a dry place, for one to two days. The sugar-coated fruits will keep much longer. To skin pistachio nuts, blanch them in boiling water for 1 minute, drain them thoroughly, then rub them vigorously in a towel.*

Pecan-Chestnut Sweetmeats

Makes about 25 sweetmeats
Working (and total) time: about 1 hour and 15 minutes

Per sweetmeat:			
Calories **45**	125 g	granulated sugar	4 oz
Protein **trace**	2½ tbsp	fresh orange juice	2½ tbsp
Cholesterol **0mg**	½ tsp	grated orange rind	½ tsp
Total fat **1g**	7.5 cm	piece cinnamon stick	3 inch
Saturated fat **trace**	60 g	shelled pecan nuts (about 50 halves)	2 oz
Sodium **5mg**		**Chestnut purée**	
	125 g	chestnuts, peeled (page 51)	4 oz
	30 g	light brown sugar	1 oz
	1 tbsp	fresh orange juice	1 tbsp
	½ tsp	grated orange rind	½ tsp
	¼ tsp	ground cinnamon	¼ tsp
	1 tbsp	brandy	1 tbsp

Dissolve the granulated sugar in the orange juice over a gentle heat, add the rind and cinnamon, and bring to the boil. Continue to boil gently until a light caramel is produced, or until the temperature on a sugar thermometer registers between 160° and 170°C (320° and 338°F). Remove the pan from the heat and place it, briefly, in a large pan of cold water to arrest the cooking process, then set it in hot water to keep the caramel fluid. Immediately coat the pecan halves in the caramel by spearing their flat sides with a skewer and dipping them into the syrup; as soon as each half is coated, use a lightly oiled fork to remove it from the skewer on to non-stick parchment paper or a lightly oiled baking sheet. Leave them to harden.

To make the chestnut purée, put the chestnuts into a pan of boiling water, return the water to the boil, then reduce the heat and simmer gently until the chestnuts begin to break apart — 20 to 30 minutes. Drain in a sieve or colander. Prepare a light syrup by boiling together the brown sugar and orange juice for 2 to 3 minutes. Process the chestnuts to a powder in a food processor or blender, or press them through a fine-meshed sieve. Mix them with the syrup, orange rind, cinnamon and brandy to obtain a creamy consistency.

Sandwich pairs of pecan halves together with a little of the chestnut purée and place them in petits fours cases. Serve while the nuts are still glossy — within a day of making them.

EDITOR'S NOTE: *The caramel may crystallize while the nuts are being dipped. If this happens, you will have to make another pan of caramel.*

Maple Sweetmeats

Makes 30 sweetmeats
Working time: about 30 minutes
Total time: about 1 hour and 30 minutes (includes chilling)

Per sweetmeat:			
Calories **35**	90 g	dried apricots	3 oz
Protein **trace**	125 g	stoned fresh dates	4 oz
Cholesterol **0mg**	90 g	stoned prunes	3 oz
Total fat **2g**	60 g	sultanas	2 oz
Saturated fat **1g**	2 tbsp	maple syrup	2 tbsp
Sodium **10mg**	100 g	desiccated coconut	3½ oz
	2 tsp	cocoa powder	2 tsp

Put the apricots, dates, prunes, sultanas and maple syrup into a food processor and blend until a sticky paste is formed. Turn the mixture out into a mixing bowl and add 90 g (3 oz) of the coconut. Mix the ingredients by hand to make a soft, but not sticky, paste.

Divide the fruit paste into 30 equal pieces, then roll each piece into a smooth ball. Place the remaining coconut in a small dish and put the cocoa powder in another. Roll half of the fruit-paste balls in the coconut to coat them evenly, then roll the remaining balls in the cocoa powder.

Place the sweetmeats in petits fours cases and refrigerate them for about 1 hour. Serve chilled.

EDITOR'S NOTE: *If you do not have a food processor, pass the fruits through the fine blade of a mincer; add the maple syrup with the coconut.*

Chocolate Rum Cups

Makes 12 cups
Working time: about 30 minutes
Total time: about 1 hour

Per cup:
Calories **105**
Protein **2g**
Cholesterol **trace**
Total fat **5g**
Saturated fat **3g**
Sodium **5mg**

60 g	plain chocolate, broken into pieces	2 oz
12	shelled hazelnuts, toasted and skinned (page 29)	12
	Chocolate rum filling	
125 g	plain chocolate, broken into pieces	4 oz
1 tbsp	dark rum	1 tbsp
60 g	fromage frais	2 oz

First make the chocolate cups. Melt the chocolate in a heatproof bowl over a pan of simmering water until it is smooth but not runny; do not allow the chocolate to become too hot or it will be very liquid and difficult to work with. Coat the insides of 12 confectionery cases with a double layer of melted chocolate as demonstrated on the right. Chill the chocolate cups while you prepare the filling.

To make the filling, melt the chocolate in a heatproof bowl over a pan of simmering water. Remove the bowl from the heat, stir in the rum and *fromage frais* and mix to a smooth paste. Leave the filling to cool until it is firm, stirring it occasionally, then transfer it to a piping bag fitted with a 1 cm (½ inch) star nozzle.

Carefully peel away the confectionery cases from the chocolate cups, and pipe a whirl of the filling into each cup. Place a hazelnut on top of each whirl.

Making Chocolate Cups

LINING CONFECTIONERY CASES. Melt chocolate in a heatproof bowl over simmering water until smooth but not yet runny. Spoon about ½ teaspoon into a foil, or a double-thickness paper, confectionery case. Using a teaspoon handle, spread the chocolate evenly over the base and up the sides of the case (above), then set aside to firm up. When all the cases have been lined, chill them for 10 to 15 minutes, then repeat the process to add a second, thinner, layer of chocolate. Chill for 20 to 30 minutes, until firmly set.

Soft-Centred Chocolate Cups

Makes 30 cups
Working time: about 1 hour
Total time: about 1 hour and 30 minutes

Per cup:			
150 g	plain chocolate, broken into pieces	5 oz
2	passion fruits, halved	2
30 g	fresh raspberries	1 oz
2 tsp	powdered gelatine	2 tsp
200 g	thick Greek yogurt	7 oz
2 tbsp	icing sugar	2 tbsp
1 tbsp	Marsala	1 tbsp
1 tbsp	kirsch	1 tbsp
	slivers of fresh fruit (cherries, oranges, grapes, kiwi fruit, raspberries or peaches), to decorate	

Per cup:
Calories **35**
Protein **1g**
Cholesterol **0mg**
Total fat **2g**
Saturated fat **1g**
Sodium **10mg**

To make the chocolate cups, melt the chocolate in a heatproof bowl over a pan of simmering water until it is smooth but not runny; do not allow the chocolate to become too hot or it will be very liquid and difficult to work with. Coat the insides of 30 confectionery cases with a double layer of melted chocolate as demonstrated opposite. Chill the chocolate cups while you prepare the filling.

Scoop the pulp out of the passion fruits and press it through a nylon sieve into a bowl. Discard the seeds and reserve the juice. Press the raspberries through the sieve into a second bowl; discard the seeds and reserve the purée.

Sprinkle the gelatine over 2 tablespoons of water in a small bowl. Leave to soften for 2 minutes, then place the bowl over a saucepan of simmering water and stir until the gelatine has completely dissolved.

Put half the yogurt into a bowl and stir in the passion fruit juice, 1 tablespoon of the icing sugar, the Marsala and half the gelatine solution. In a separate bowl, mix the rest of the yogurt with the raspberry purée, kirsch, and the remaining icing sugar and gelatine solution.

Carefully peel away the confectionery cases from the chocolate cups. Using a teaspoon, fill half the chocolate cups with the passion fruit filling and the other half with the raspberry filling. Decorate the filled cups with slivers of fresh fruit and chill them until the filling has set — at least 30 minutes. Serve the cups on the day they are filled.

EDITOR'S NOTE: *Unfilled, the chocolate cups may be stored in an airtight container in the refrigerator for several days.*

Chestnut Boats

Makes 20 boats
Working time: about 1 hour and 15 minutes
Total time: about 1 hour and 45 minutes

Per boat:
Calories **55**
Protein **1g**
Cholesterol **0mg**
Total fat **2g**
Saturated fat **1g**
Sodium **10mg**

125 g	plain chocolate, broken into pieces	4 oz
175 g	fresh chestnuts, peeled (page 51)	6 oz
30 cl	skimmed milk	½ pint
½	vanilla pod	½
1 tbsp	clear honey	1 tbsp
3 tbsp	thick Greek yogurt	3 tbsp
½ tsp	pure vanilla extract	½ tsp
½ tsp	grated orange rind	½ tsp
1	orange, rind only, julienned, blanched for 1 minute and drained	1

To make the boats, melt the chocolate in a heatproof bowl over a pan of simmering water until it is smooth but not runny; do not allow the chocolate to become too hot or it will be very liquid and difficult to work with. Follow the method for making chocolate cups (page 122), using 5 cm (2 inch) plain barquette moulds in-stead of confectionery cases. Chill the boats in the refrigerator while you make the chestnut filling.

Put the peeled chestnuts into a small saucepan with the milk and vanilla pod; if necessary, top up the liquid with water to cover the chestnuts. Bring to the boil, then reduce the heat and simmer gently until the chestnuts begin to break apart — 20 to 30 minutes. Drain well, discarding the milk (the vanilla pod may be washed, dried and used again). Process the chestnuts to a soft powder in a food processor or blender, or press them through a fine-meshed sieve. Put the pow-dered chestnuts into a bowl and stir in the honey, yogurt, vanilla extract and grated orange rind, to make a smooth cream. Spoon the mixture into a piping bag fitted with a 5 mm (¼ inch) star nozzle.

Using a small, sharp knife, loosen and remove the chocolate boats from the moulds. Pipe a little of the chestnut cream decoratively into each one. Arrange strips of rind over the chestnut cream. Serve the chocolate boats within 2 hours of filling.

EDITOR'S NOTE: *The chocolate boats and the chestnut cream may be made a day or two in advance and stored separately in the refrigerator.*

Dried Fruit Nuggets

Makes 24 nuggets
Working time: about 45 minutes
Total time: about 4 hours

Per nugget:
Calories **65**
Protein **trace**
Cholesterol **0mg**
Total fat **1g**
Saturated fat **trace**
Sodium **10mg**

200 g	granulated sugar	7 oz
7.5 cm	strip lemon rind	3 inch
7.5 cm	piece cinnamon stick	3 inch
3	cloves	3
3	cardamom pods, lightly crushed	3
1	blade mace	1
½ tsp	mixed spice	½ tsp
60 g	ready-to-eat dried apricots, cut into 5 mm (¼ inch) dice	2 oz
60 g	dried pears, cut into 5 mm (¼ inch) dice	2 oz
60 g	dried pineapple, cut into 5 mm (¼ inch) dice	2 oz
60 g	dried figs, cut into 5 mm (¼ inch) dice	2 oz
30 g	red glacé cherries, quartered	1 oz
60 g	plain chocolate, broken into pieces	2 oz

Dissolve the sugar in 15 cl (¼ pint) of water in a medium-sized heavy-bottomed saucepan over gentle heat; brush down any sugar crystals that stick to the sides of the pan with a bristle pastry brush dipped in hot water. Add the lemon rind, cinnamon, cloves, cardamom, mace and mixed spice and simmer gently for 5 minutes. Remove the rind and whole spices with a slotted spoon and discard them.

Increase the heat, place a sugar thermometer in the pan and bring the solution to a rapid boil. When the sugar reaches a temperature of 118°C (244°F), reduce the heat and add the diced apricots, pears, pineapple and figs. Stir once, then cook the fruit gently for 5 minutes without stirring; the temperature should rise slightly during this period, but do not allow it to exceed 125°C (257°F) or the fruit may set too hard. Add the cherries and remove the pan from the heat.

Using a teaspoon and working quickly, lift spoonfuls of fruit out of the syrup and drop them in nuggets on to a sheet of non-stick parchment paper. Allow the nuggets to cool at room temperature for at least 3 hours. When they are cool but still pliable, round them off with your fingers and put them on a fresh piece of parchment paper, ready for decorating with chocolate.

Melt the chocolate in a heatproof bowl over a pan of simmering water. Fold a greaseproof paper piping bag *(page 13)* and fill it with the chocolate. Fold down the top of the bag, cut off the tip, and dribble zigzags of fine chocolate piping over the nuggets. Leave the chocolate to set for about 15 minutes before serving the nuggets.

EDITOR'S NOTE: *When the fruit mixture is spooned out into nuggets, the sugar syrup in the pan will tend to harden and crystallize; if it becomes too difficult to work with, reheat the mixture gently to melt the sugar again. The decorated nuggets may be stored in an airtight container for a few days, layered between sheets of parchment paper.*

Chocolate-Dipped Stuffed Prunes

THIS RECIPE PROVIDES AN IDEAL OPPORTUNITY TO USE UP
GENOESE SPONGE TRIMMINGS THAT MAY BE LEFT OVER FROM
SEVERAL OF THE RECIPES IN CHAPTER 2.

Makes 18 stuffed prunes
Working time: about 1 hour
Total time: about 3 hours (includes setting)

Per prune:
Calories **100**
Protein **1g**
Cholesterol **0mg**
Total fat **1g**
Saturated fat **trace**
Sodium **20mg**

100 g	granulated sugar	3½ oz
15 cm	piece cinnamon stick	6 inch
1	vanilla pod	1
350 g	large prunes	12 oz
60 g	genoese sponge (recipe, page 11), or other plain sponge cake	2 oz
60 g	shelled walnuts, lightly toasted and ground	2 oz
4 tbsp	Armagnac or cognac	4 tbsp
½ tsp	pure vanilla extract	½ tsp
75 g	white chocolate, broken into pieces	2½ oz

Place the sugar in a saucepan with ¼ litre (8 fl oz) of water and heat gently until the sugar has dissolved. Add the cinnamon and vanilla pod, bring to the boil, then reduce the heat and simmer for 5 minutes. Add the prunes and simmer for a further 5 minutes. Using a slotted spoon, remove 18 large, well-shaped prunes and allow them to cool on a plate, then stone them carefully and open up the cavities to receive the filling. Meanwhile, continue simmering the remaining prunes until they are very tender — 20 to 40 minutes — then transfer them to a plate to cool. Discard the syrup.

Next, make the filling. Stone the soft-cooked prunes and place them in a food processor with the sponge, ground walnuts, Armagnac and vanilla extract. Process to a smooth purée. Using a teaspoon, press the filling into the prunes, and bring the sides of each prune round the filling.

Melt the chocolate in a heatproof bowl over a pan of simmering water, until it is smooth and just free of lumps but still quite thick. Dip and turn each prune in the chocolate to coat one end. Arrange the prunes, filled-side up, on a sheet of non-stick parchment paper and leave them until the chocolate has set. Serve them in petits fours cases.

EDITOR'S NOTE: The stuffed prunes may be stored for several days in the refrigerator, layered between sheets of parchment paper in an airtight container. To toast walnuts, put them under a hot grill for 2 minutes, or until they begin to darken, shaking them constantly.

Glazed Fruits

Makes about 45 glazed fruits
Working (and total) time: about 30 minutes

Per fruit:
Calories **15**
Protein **trace**
Cholesterol **0mg**
Total fat **0g**
Saturated fat **0g**
Sodium **trace**

8	*seedless black grapes*	8
8	*seedless green grapes*	8
8	*small strawberries, hulled*	8
1	*satsuma, peeled, segmented, all white pith removed from segments*	1
6	*raspberries*	6
6	*Cape gooseberries*	6
175 g	*granulated sugar*	6 oz

Pierce each piece of fruit with a cocktail stick. Line a large baking sheet with non-stick parchment paper.

Place the sugar and 4 tablespoons of water in a small, heavy-bottomed saucepan. Set the pan over a medium heat and stir the mixture gently with a wooden spoon to dissolve the sugar. Brush down any sugar crystals stuck to the sides of the pan with a bristle pastry brush dipped in hot water. Warm a sugar thermometer in a jug of hot water and place it in the pan. Bring the syrup to the boil and boil it rapidly until it reaches the small crack stage, when the temperature on the thermometer registers between 132° and 143°C (270° and 290°F). At this temperature, when a little syrup is dropped from a skewer into a bowl of iced water and then removed and stretched gently between the fingers, it will separate into strands that are hard but still elastic.

Remove the syrup from the heat. Working quickly, dip the pieces of fruit, one at a time, into the syrup, then put them on the prepared baking sheet to cool and harden. Allow the syrup to set for at least 5 minutes before removing the cocktail sticks. Place each fruit in a decorative confectionery case to serve.

EDITOR'S NOTE: *Prepare the fruits as near as possible to serving time and keep them in a dry place. The sugar coating on the fruits quickly becomes sticky in a damp or humid atmosphere.*

4 *After expanding five-fold in only a few seconds, microwaved meringues are sandwiched together with a light almond pastry cream (recipe, opposite).*

Patisserie from the Microwave

Clean, efficient and versatile, a microwave oven can be an invaluable tool for making patisserie. Its use need not be restricted to the recipes on the following pages, for though it is not suited to baking shortcrust or choux doughs, it is ideal for preparing many individual elements of a recipe before final assembly. Many processes, such as melting chocolate and gelatine, are not only quicker in the microwave but also more convenient, since no saucepans are required.

When cooked in a microwave, a sponge mixture will rise to an amazing height in seconds without darkening in colour, making it the perfect partner for pastel creams and mousses. Because of the speed of the process, follow the cooking times closely. The sponge will be ready when it is springy to the touch, slightly shrunk away from the sides of the dish and still a little moist on top. This moisture will evaporate if the sponge is left to stand, so do not be tempted to return it to the oven or it will dry out.

Because microwaves do not burn food, pastry cream can be cooked until every trace of raw cornflour has disappeared without fear of scorching the custard. Regular stirring with a wire whisk is all that is required to keep the custard smooth. Fruit cooked in a microwave retains its flavour and colour. To preserve its shape, cook it in a single layer in a shallow dish, and to avoid moisture loss, cover the dish with plastic film made especially for use in the microwave. Always pull a corner of the film back to prevent too much steam from building up.

Traditional meringues cannot be baked in a microwave oven, but the amaretto meringues on the left, with a large ratio of icing sugar to egg white, have been specially created for this cooking method. A small amount of mixture — about ½ teaspoon — cooks to a large, fluffy meringue, so leave plenty of space around each one when baking them.

All the recipes in this section have been tested in 650-watt and 700-watt ovens. Although power settings may vary among different ovens, the recipes use "high" to indicate 100 per cent power, "medium" for 50 per cent power, and "medium low" or "defrost" for 30 per cent power. The recipes also give instructions for turning the cakes so that they rise evenly, but these directions can be ignored if your microwave oven has an automatic turntable.

Amaretto Meringues

MICROWAVED MERINGUES ARE VERY DIFFERENT FROM THOSE COOKED IN A CONVENTIONAL OVEN: THEY ARE SOFT AND FRAGILE, AND DISSOLVE IN THE MOUTH WHEN EATEN.

Makes 32 meringues
Working (and total) time: about 20 minutes

Per meringue:
Calories **65**
Protein **1g**
Cholesterol **15mg**
Total fat **2g**
Saturated fat **trace**
Sodium **10mg**

1	egg white	1
300 g	icing sugar	10 oz
⅛ tsp	pure almond extract	⅛ tsp
30 g	flaked almonds	1 oz
1 tbsp	amaretto liqueur	1 tbsp
30 cl	pastry cream (page 11 or 130)	½ pint

Put the egg white into a bowl, sift in the icing sugar and add the almond extract. Stir the mixture until it is very stiff and firm; if it is sticky, add a little more icing sugar — about 1 teaspoon.

Using your fingers, shape the mixture into 64 small balls of about ½ teaspoon of mixture each. Place eight balls, spaced well apart, in a circle on non-stick parchment paper. Using your thumb, lightly flatten each ball, and press a few flaked almonds into the top of each. Microwave the balls on high for 1 minute, giving the paper a quarter turn every 20 seconds; the meringues will increase in size until they measure about 6 cm (2 ½ inches), and should hold their shape when cooked — if they collapse when the oven door is opened, cook them for a further 20 seconds.

Remove the meringues from the oven, allow to cool for 1 minute, then carefully lift them off the paper and place them on a wire rack to finish cooling. Continue preparing and cooking the balls in batches of eight.

Stir the amaretto into the pastry cream. Using a round-bladed knife, spread about 1 tablespoon of flavoured pastry cream on to the flat surface of a meringue, then gently press the flat surface of a second meringue into the cream. Arrange the filled meringues on a serving plate and serve them immediately.

EDITOR'S NOTE: *The uncooked meringue mixture can be wrapped in plastic film and kept in the refrigerator for up to three months. Cooked meringues can be stored in an airtight tin for two weeks and filled with pastry cream as required.*

Apple Castles

Makes 6 castles
Working time: about 30 minutes
Total time: about 1 hour and 30 minutes

Per castle:		1	egg	1

Per castle:
Calories **160**
Protein **3g**
Cholesterol **80mg**
Total fat **2g**
Saturated fat **trace**
Sodium **20mg**

1	egg	1
90g	caster sugar	3 oz
60 g	plain flour	2 oz
4	dessert apples	4
1	orange, juice only	1
8 cl	pastry cream (page 11 or box, below)	3 fl oz
2 tbsp	Grand Marnier	2 tbsp
1 tsp	powdered gelatine	1 tsp
6	mint sprigs, to decorate	6

Line the base of an 18 by 10 cm (7 by 4 inch) shallow baking dish with greaseproof paper.

To make the sponge, whisk together the egg and 60 g (2 oz) of the sugar until the mixture is very thick and pale and falls from the whisk in a ribbon trail. Sift the flour lightly over the surface of the mixture, then fold it in gently with a metal spoon. Pour the batter into the prepared dish, tipping the dish to distribute it evenly. Microwave on high until the sides of the sponge begin to pull away from the dish but the top is still slightly moist — 50 to 60 seconds. When cool, turn out on to a board and remove the paper.

Peel the apples, then core them with an apple corer, keeping them whole. With a sharp knife, cut them horizontally into thin, circular slices. Keep six small slices whole; cut the remainder in half. Put them in a shallow round dish, and sprinkle them with the remaining sugar and with the orange juice. Cover the dish with plastic film, leaving a corner open, and microwave on high until the slices are tender but still retain their shape — 3 to 4 minutes. Cool slightly, then drain the juices into a small bowl and set aside.

Line the bases of six dariole moulds with grease-proof paper. Place a small whole apple slice in the bottom of each; if the slices will not fit, then cut them to size. Line the sides of each mould with the halved apple slices, using four or five slices per mould. Roughly chop any remaining slices and stir them into the pastry cream with half of the Grand Marnier.

Sprinkle the gelatine over the reserved apple juices, and leave to stand for 2 minutes. Heat the mixture on high until the gelatine has dissolved — about 30 seconds — then thoroughly incorporate into the pastry cream. Divide the mixture among the six moulds.

Cut six discs out of the sponge to fit snugly inside the apple slices, on top of pastry cream. Sprinkle the remaining Grand Marnier over the sponge discs. Chill the moulds for 1 hour, then unmould them and remove the paper. Serve decorated with a mint sprig.

Microwave Pastry Cream

Makes about 30 cl (½ pint)
Working time: about 20 minutes
Total time: about 1 hour and 45 minutes (includes chilling)

2	egg yolks	2
30 g	caster sugar	1 oz
30 g	plain flour, sifted	1 oz
15 g	cornflour, sifted	½ oz
30 cl	skimmed milk	½ pint
1 tsp	pure vanilla extract	1 tsp
2 tbsp	thick Greek yogurt	2 tbsp
1	egg white	1

Put the egg yolks and half the sugar into a mixing bowl. Whisk them together until thick, then carefully fold in the flour and cornflour. Gradually whisk in the milk and vanilla extract to form a smooth batter. Microwave on high for 3 to 3½ minutes, whisking every minute; when cooked the mixture should form a thick, smooth custard, with no taste of raw flour remaining. Closely cover the surface of the custard with plastic film, to prevent a skin from forming. Allow the custard to cool for about 10 minutes, then refrigerate until it is almost, but not quite, cold — 15 to 20 minutes.

Whisk the custard until it is smooth, then whisk in the yogurt. Whisk the egg white until stiff, then whisk in the remaining sugar until the mixture is shiny. Gradually fold the egg white into the custard, using a metal spoon. Cover the pastry cream with plastic film and chill for at least 1 hour.

EDITOR'S NOTE: *The pastry cream may be stored in the refrigerator for up to two days.*

Banana Diamonds

Makes 12 diamonds
Working time: about 40 minutes
Total time: about 1 hour and 15 minutes

Per diamond:
Calories **190**
Protein **4g**
Cholesterol **20mg**
Total fat **6g**
Saturated fat **1g**
Sodium **180mg**

175 g	wholemeal flour	6 oz
½ tsp	bicarbonate of soda	½ tsp
125 g	light brown sugar	4 oz
4 tbsp	skimmed milk	4 tbsp
2	ripe bananas, mashed	2
4 tbsp	safflower or sunflower oil	4 tbsp
1	egg	1
½ tsp	baking powder	½ tsp
½ tsp	pure vanilla extract	½ tsp
2 tbsp	icing sugar, to decorate	2 tbsp
Cheese filling		
200 g	low-fat soft cheese	7 oz
3 tbsp	icing sugar	3 tbsp
3 ½ tbsp	fresh orange juice	3 ½ tbsp
1 tsp	mixed spice	1 tsp

Line the base of a 28 by 18 cm (11 by 7 inch) rectangular dish with non-stick parchment paper.

Put the flour and bicarbonate of soda into a large bowl, mix in the light brown sugar, then add the milk, bananas, oil, egg, baking powder and vanilla extract. Beat the mixture until smooth, then turn it into the lined dish and microwave on medium for 6 minutes, giving the dish a half turn every 2 minutes. Increase the power to high and microwave until the cake is springy to the touch but still moist — 4 to 5 minutes. Remove the cake from the oven and leave in the dish for 3 minutes before inverting it on to a wire rack. Remove the paper and leave to cool.

To make the filling, put the cheese, sugar, orange juice and mixed spice in a bowl and mix thoroughly.

Place the cake, right-side up, on a work surface and trim round the edges to make a neat rectangle. Using a sharp, long-bladed knife, cut horizontally through the cake to give two equal layers. Spread the filling evenly over the bottom layer of the cake. Replace the top layer and cut the cake lengthwise into three equal strips. Cut each strip diagonally into four diamond shapes. (There will be two small triangles left over from the ends of each strip.)

Using stiff paper, cut out a diamond-shaped template the size of one of the banana diamonds. With a pencil, draw a large X across the middle, making four small diamonds. Cut out two facing diamonds, taking care to leave the other two joined in the centre. Place the template on one of the banana diamonds and sprinkle it with the icing sugar. Remove the template and repeat with the rest of the cakes.

Chocolate Boxes

Makes 18 boxes
Working time: about 1 hour
Total time: about 1 hour and 30 minutes

Per box:			
Calories **70**	1	egg	1
Protein **2g**	45g	caster sugar	1½ oz
Cholesterol **40mg**	45 g	plain flour	1½ oz
Total fat **3g**	60 g	plain chocolate, broken into pieces	2 oz
Saturated fat **1g**	1 tbsp	kirsch	1 tbsp
Sodium **20mg**	30 cl	pastry cream (page 11 or 130)	½ pint
	5	strawberries, hulled and quartered lengthwise	5

Line the base of an 18 by 10 by 4 cm (7 by 4 by 1½ inch) dish with greaseproof paper. Put the egg and sugar into a mixing bowl and whisk until the mixture is very thick and pale, and falls from the whisk in a ribbon trail. Sift the flour lightly over the whisked mixture, then fold it in gently with a metal spoon. Pour the batter into the prepared dish, tipping the dish to distribute it evenly. Microwave on high for about 50 seconds (the top of the sponge should still be slightly moist). Set the sponge aside to cool in the dish.

Meanwhile, start making the chocolate squares.

Grease a 30 by 15 cm (12 by 6 inch) tin and line it with waxed paper. Place the chocolate in a small bowl and microwave on medium for 2½ to 3 minutes, until the chocolate has melted, then pour it into the prepared tin, spread it evenly with a metal spatula and leave to set in a cool place — about 30 minutes.

Invert the cooled sponge on to a board and remove the paper. Using a sharp knife, trim all four sides to obtain neat straight edges. Then cut the sponge rectangle into 18 squares slightly smaller than 2.5 cm (1 inch), and discard the excess. Cut the chocolate into 72 squares measuring 2.5 cm (1 inch) each (page 12).

Stir the kirsch into the pastry cream. Using a round-bladed knife, spread a little of the pastry cream on the sides of the sponges and press a chocolate square to each side. Transfer the remaining pastry cream to a piping bag fitted with a medium star nozzle. Pipe two lines of cream across each box and place a strawberry quarter on top.

EDITOR'S NOTE: These boxes may be stored in the refrigerator for four or five days; do not top with fruit until ready to serve. The strawberries can be replaced by other fresh seasonal fruits such as cherries, raspberries, tangerine segments or kiwi fruit slices, or by a colourful combination of several.

Peach and Passion Fruit Petits Fours

Makes 36 petits fours
Working time: about 1 hour
Total time: about 3 hours

Per petit four:			
Calories **25**	15 g	unsalted butter	½ oz
Protein **2g**	2	eggs	2
Cholesterol **15mg**	60 g	caster sugar	2 oz
Total fat **1g**	60 g	plain flour	2 oz
Saturated fat **trace**	¼ tsp	baking powder	¼ tsp
Sodium **25mg**	½ tbsp	fresh lemon juice	½ tbsp
	2 tbsp	raspberry jam without added sugar, sieved, to decorate	2 tbsp
	5 cm	stick angelica, sliced diagonally into diamond shapes, to decorate	2 inch

Peach filling		
2	peaches, blanched for 30 seconds, peeled, stoned, thinly sliced and covered in acidulated water	2
30 g	icing sugar	1 oz
1 tsp	arrowroot	1 tsp
1 tbsp	fresh lemon juice	1 tbsp
15 g	powdered gelatine	½ oz
100 g	quark	3½ oz

Passion fruit icing		
4	passion fruits	4
125 g	icing sugar, sifted	4 oz

Line the base of a 20 cm (8 inch) square microwave dish, at least 4 cm (1½ inches) deep, with non-stick parchment paper.

Place the butter in a small bowl and microwave on low for about 1 minute, until melted. Set aside to cool. Put the eggs and sugar into a mixing bowl and whisk until the mixture is very thick and pale and falls from the whisk in a ribbon trail. Sift the flour and baking powder lightly over the whisked mixture, fold it in gently using a metal spoon, then carefully fold in the lemon juice and ½ tablespoon of water. Pour in the cooled butter, and fold it in quickly and thoroughly.

Pour the batter into the prepared dish and microwave on high until the sponge is well risen and the surface still appears moist — 2½ to 3 minutes; give the dish a quarter-turn every 45 seconds. Remove the cake from the oven and allow to rest until no damp patches remain on the surface of the sponge — 5 to 8 minutes. Unmould on to a wire rack covered with a layer of greaseproof paper and leave to cool.

To make the peach filling, dry the peach slices thoroughly on paper towels then place them in a bowl. Sprinkle with the icing sugar and microwave on high for 1 minute. Press the fruit through a nylon sieve into another bowl. Dissolve the arrowroot in the lemon juice and stir this into the peach purée. Microwave on medium, stirring frequently, for about 1 minute, until the purée is thick and clear. Remove and cool to room temperature — about 20 minutes.

Meanwhile, sprinkle the gelatine over 2 tablespoons of water in a small bowl. Leave to soften for 2 minutes, then microwave on high for 30 seconds until the gelatine has dissolved. Microwave the quark on low for 1 minute to bring it to room temperature. Beat the quark briefly until smooth, beat in the peach purée, then whisk in the gelatine. Place the filling in the refrigerator for 10 to 15 minutes to thicken before spreading.

Remove the parchment paper from the sponge and invert the sponge on to a board. Using a sharp, long-bladed knife, cut the sponge horizontally into three layers. Spread half the filling over the bottom layer. Set the middle layer on the filling, cover that with the remaining peach mixture and place the third sponge layer on top. Trim the edges with a sharp knife.

To make the icing, cut the passion fruits in half and, using a teaspoon, scoop the seeds and pulp into a nylon sieve set over a bowl. Press the pulp through the sieve, then discard the seeds. Blend the sugar into the juice, adding a little water if necessary to achieve a thick coating consistency. Spread the icing over the top layer of sponge with a metal spatula, then lightly score the top with the tip of a sharp knife to mark out 36 squares. Set aside until set — about 1 hour.

Before serving, fold a greaseproof paper piping bag *(page 13)* and fill it with the raspberry jam. Decorate each square with the jam and angelica diamonds. Cut into the marked squares just before serving.

EDITOR'S NOTE: *If preferred, the uncut assembly may be wrapped in plastic film and stored in the refrigerator for four or five days. It can then be cut and decorated as required.*

Chocolate and Ginger Cheesecakes

Makes 6 cheesecakes
Working time: about 30 minutes
Total time: about 3 hours (includes chilling)

Per cheesecake:
Calories **210**
Protein **10g**
Cholesterol **10mg**
Total fat **9g**
Saturated fat **5g**
Sodium **230mg**

45 g	digestive biscuits	1½ oz
75 g	plain chocolate	2½ oz
2 tsp	powdered gelatine	2 tsp
2 tbsp	clear honey	2 tbsp
30 g	crystallized ginger	1 oz
300 g	quark	10 oz
6 cl	single cream	2 fl oz
1 tsp	icing sugar, to decorate	1 tsp

Cut six circles of greaseproof paper to line the bases of six 12.5 cl (4 fl oz) ramekins, using a ramekin as a guide. Break the biscuits into pieces, and process them briefly in a food processor. Break 45 g (1½ oz) of the chocolate into a basin and microwave it on medium for 2½ to 3 minutes, until melted. Stir until smooth, then combine with the biscuit crumbs. Divide the mixture among the ramekins, lightly pressing it into the bases. Chill until firm — about 20 minutes.

Sprinkle the gelatine over 2 tablespoons of water in a bowl and leave it to soften for 2 minutes. Microwave on high for 30 seconds, to melt the gelatine. Stir in the honey and cool slightly.

Meanwhile, very finely chop the ginger in a food processor and combine it with the quark and cream. Mix together until smooth, then blend in the gelatine mixture thoroughly. Divide among the ramekins, cover with plastic film and chill for at least 2 hours, or preferably overnight, until set.

For the topping, break the remaining chocolate into a basin and microwave it on medium for 2 to 2½ minutes. Stir the chocolate until smooth, then, using a metal spatula, spread it out very thinly on a marble slab or an inverted baking sheet. Leave to cool for 3 to 4 minutes, until almost set. Push a pastry scraper under the chocolate to produce scrolls *(page 12)*.

Just before serving, slip a knife round the sides of the ramekins. Carefully unmould each cheesecake into the palm of your hand — to remove the lining paper — then place it on a board. Cover the cheesecakes with chocolate scrolls. Using a metal spatula to cover half the top of each cheesecake, sift icing sugar over the other half.

Pear and Hazelnut Galettes

Makes 8 galettes
Working time: about 30 minutes
Total time: about 1 hour

Per galette:
Calories **175**
Protein **2g**
Cholesterol **30mg**
Total fat **5g**
Saturated fat **2g**
Sodium **15mg**

2	Conference pears	2
15 cl	port	¼ pint
90 g	caster sugar	3 oz
15 g	glacé ginger, finely chopped	½ oz
6 tbsp	pastry cream (page 11 or 130)	6 tbsp
Hazelnut shortbread		
30 g	unsalted butter	1 oz
15 g	caster sugar	½ oz
45 g	plain flour	1 ½ oz
15 g	shelled hazelnuts, toasted and skinned (page 29), finely ground	½ oz

Peel the pears, cut them in half lengthwise, scoop out the cores, then cut the pears into long thin slices.

Combine the port and sugar in a 20 cm (8 inch) shallow round dish. Microwave on high for 2 minutes, then stir until the sugar has dissolved. Place the pear slices in the syrup, turning them so that they are well coated. Cover the dish with plastic film, leaving a corner open to allow steam to escape. Cook the pear slices on

high, giving the dish a quarter turn after 3 minutes, until they are tender but still hold their shape — 6 to 8 minutes. At the end of cooking, loosen the plastic film and drain the syrup into a heatproof bowl. Leave the pears to cool

Heat the syrup, without stirring, on high until it has become quite thick and smells slightly of caramel — about 7 minutes — then set it aside to cool.

Meanwhile, make the shortbread. Cream together the butter and sugar, then mix in the flour and hazelnuts to make a stiff dough. Turn the dough on to a lightly floured work surface and roll it out to a thickness of about 3 mm (⅛ inch). Using a 7.5 cm (3 inch) plain cutter, cut out eight circles. Place a sheet of non-stick parchment paper in the microwave. Put four shortbread circles on the paper and cook them on high for 2 minutes. Allow them to cool slightly, before placing them on a wire rack and cooking the second batch.

Stir the chopped ginger into the pastry cream. Spoon a little pastry cream on to each of the eight cooled shortbread circles, spreading it to within 5 mm (¼ inch) of the edge. Arrange three or four pear slices on each shortbread base, trimming the fruit to size if necessary. Place the galettes on a wire rack over a baking tray and dribble the thickened syrup over the pears. Serve immediately.

Chocolate Bombes

Makes 12 bombes
Working time: about 45 minutes
Total time: about 3 hours (includes chilling)

Per bombe:
Calories **150**
Protein **5g**
Cholesterol **15mg**
Total fat **9g**
Saturated fat **5g**
Sodium **140mg**

250 g	low-fat cottage cheese	8 oz
30 g	caster sugar	1 oz
4 tbsp	whipping cream	4 tbsp
½	lemon, grated rind only	½
30 g	glacé cherries, finely chopped	1 oz
30 g	glacé ginger, finely chopped	1 oz
1 tbsp	Tia Maria	1 tbsp
30 g	shelled walnuts, finely chopped	1 oz
2.5 cm	cube crystallized ginger, chopped, to decorate	1 inch
Chocolate coating		
90 g	plain chocolate	3 oz
45 g	unsalted butter	1½ oz

Sieve the cottage cheese into a bowl, add the caster sugar and whipping cream, and whisk with an electric mixer until the mixture is very light. Divide the mixture evenly between two bowls. Add the grated lemon rind, glacé cherries and chopped ginger to the cheese mixture in one bowl. Stir the Tia Maria and chopped walnuts into the other bowl. Set both bowls aside.

Use plastic egg boxes as moulds for the bombes. Line 12 moulds with pieces of plastic film. Distribute the glacé cherry and ginger mixture evenly among the moulds, smooth the surfaces, then spoon on the nut and Tia Maria mixture and smooth the tops again. Chill the bombes for 2 hours.

To make the coating, put the chocolate and butter into a small bowl and microwave them on medium until the chocolate has melted — 3 to 4 minutes. Stir the mixture until it is smooth, then leave it to cool until almost beginning to set.

Unmould the bombes on to a board and remove the plastic film. Slide a metal spatula under one bombe, hold it over the bowl of melted chocolate and carefully spoon the mixture over the bombe, spreading it with a knife to ensure an even coating. Set the bombe on a wire rack and score the surface of the chocolate coating with the tines of a fork. Coat the remaining bombes in the same way. Decorate each one with a piece of crystallized ginger.

Serve the bombes when the chocolate coating has completely set — 10 to 15 minutes.

EDITOR'S NOTE: *The bombes may be stored in the refrigerator for up to four days.*

Candied Fruit Sticks

Makes: 36 sticks
Working time: about 45 minutes
Total time: about 2 days and 2 hours
(includes 2 days' soaking)

Per stick:	1	lemon	1
Calories **51**	1	orange	1
Protein **trace**			
Cholesterol **0mg**	1 tsp	bicarbonate of soda	1 tsp
Total fat **1g**	350 g	caster sugar	12 oz
Saturated fat **trace**	60 g	milk chocolate	2 oz
Sodium **2mg**	45 g	plain chocolate	1 ½ oz

Wash the fruit thoroughly, slit through the peel with a sharp knife to divide it into quarters, then carefully remove the whole quarters of peel.

Place the bicarbonate of soda in a bowl and stir in 60 cl (1 pint) of boiling water. Immerse the peel, weight it down with a saucer, and leave it to soften for 20 minutes. Drain and rinse the peel, then cut lengthwise into 5 mm (¼ inch) sticks. Place the sticks in a bowl with 45 cl (¾ pint) of cold water. Cover the bowl with plastic film, leaving one edge open, and microwave on high for 25 minutes, stirring once, until the peel is tender. Drain the cooked peel.

Combine 250 g (8 oz) of the caster sugar with 30 cl (½ pint) of cold water in a 1.75 litre (3 pint) mixing bowl. (Do not use a smaller bowl or the hot sugar syrup will boil over in the microwave oven.) Microwave the mixture on high for 8 minutes, stirring two or three times, until the sugar has completely dissolved. Immerse the

peel in the syrup, cover and leave to soak for two days.

Remove the sticks from the syrup with a slotted spoon and place them on a plate. Add the remaining sugar to the syrup and microwave it on high for about 6 minutes, stirring once, until the sugar has dissolved and the syrup is boiling. Return the sticks to the boiling syrup and microwave them on high for 10 to 13 minutes, until they look translucent. Watch them carefully towards the end of the cooking time — they can easily burn if left too long.

Place a sheet of non-stick parchment paper in the microwave. Drain the sticks well and spread them out in a single layer on the paper. Microwave on medium low for 24 minutes, moving the strips every 6 minutes to ensure even drying. The sticks are ready when they feel just dry and look sugary. Leave to cool.

Break the milk chocolate into a bowl and microwave it on medium for 2½ to 3 minutes, until melted. Stir it well until smooth, then hold an orange stick in your fingers and half dip it in the chocolate. Set the coated stick on a sheet of non-stick parchment paper. Continue until all the orange sticks have been dipped. Melt the plain chocolate and half dip the lemon sticks in the same way. Leave the sticks to set for 10 minutes.

EDITOR'S NOTE: *The candied orange and lemon sticks can also be left uncoated, and either eaten as a sweetmeat or chopped and used to flavour biscuits and cakes. Store them in an airtight tin for up to three months; once dipped in chocolate, the sticks should be stored in the refrigerator for up to three weeks only.*

Glossary

Amaretto: an almond-flavoured liqueur.
Angelica: the stalk of the angelica plant that has been candied in sugar syrup. Cut into delicate shapes, it is used as a decoration.
Armagnac: a dry brandy, often more strongly flavoured than cognac, from the Armagnac district of south-west France.
Arrowroot: a tasteless, starchy, white powder refined from the root of a tropical plant; it is used to thicken purées and sauces. Unlike flour, it is transparent when cooked.
Baking powder: a raising agent that releases carbon dioxide during baking, causing cake or biscuit batter to rise. Ordinary baking powders, as used in these recipes, have a high sodium content, but low-sodium baking powder is available for people on restricted-sodium diets.
Bicarbonate of soda: a raising agent in cake-making, it is activated when combined with an acidic ingredient such as vinegar or black treacle.
Brown sugars: ranging in colour from pale beige to dark brown, brown sugars are often prepared by purifying raw cane sugar to some degree. Alternatively, brown sugar is made from fully refined white sugar mingled with molasses. Nutritionally, brown sugars have only a fractional advantage over white sugars but they are valued for their stronger flavour.
Calorie (or kilocalorie): a precise measure of the energy food supplies when it is broken down for use in the body.
Calvados: an apple brandy made in the Normandy region of France.
Cape gooseberry: a small, tart fruit enclosed in a delicate papery husk. It can be eaten raw or cooked.
Caramelize: to heat sugar, or a food naturally rich in sugar such as fruit, until the sugar turns brown and syrupy.
Cardamom: the bittersweet, aromatic dried seeds or whole pods of a plant in the ginger family. Cardamom seeds may be used whole or ground.
Chocolate: the refined product of the cocoa bean. For baking and confectionery, select good-quality, dark chocolate, which contains a high proportion — about 50 per cent — of cocoa butter and cocoa solids and little or no vegetable fat.
Cholesterol: a waxlike substance that is manufactured in the human body and also found in foods of animal origin. Although a certain amount of cholesterol is necessary for proper body functioning, an excess can accumulate in the arteries, contributing to heart disease. See also Monounsaturated fats; Polyunsaturated fats; Saturated fats.
Cocoa powder: the result of pulverizing roasted cocoa beans, then removing most of the fat, or cocoa butter.
Cointreau: a liqueur prepared from the zest of sweet and bitter oranges in a white spirit base.
Confectionery cases: small paper cases for holding confectionery and petits fours. If they are to be used to bake petits fours in, they should be of unwaxed paper.
Cornflour: a starchy white powder made from corn kernels and used to thicken many puddings and sauces. Like arrowroot, it is transparent when cooked and makes a more efficient thickener than flour. When

cooked conventionally, a liquid containing cornflour must be stirred constantly in the early stages to prevent lumps from forming.
Cornmeal: finely ground dried maize.
Cottage cheese: a low-fat soft cheese with a mild flavour and a non-uniform texture. It is made from skimmed milk, but the cottage cheese used in this book has added cream to give it a fat content of 4 per cent.
Crystallized ginger: (also called candied ginger): the spicy, rootlike stems of ginger preserved dry with sugar. Crystallized ginger should not be confused with preserved stem ginger, which is preserved in syrup — the two are not always interchangeable.
Curd cheese: any soft cheese made from separated milk curds. The medium and low-fat soft cheeses used in this book contain 12 and 5 per cent fat respectively.
Dates: the fruit of the date palm, dates can be bought fresh or dried. When dried dates are specified, choose plump unstoned dates in preference to pressed slab dates.
Demerara sugar: a large-crystal brown sugar. See also Brown sugars.
Dietary fibre: a plant-cell material that passes undigested through the human body, but promotes healthy digestion of other food matter.
Eau de vie: a clear white spirit distilled from fruit such as pears or raspberries.
Fat: a basic component of many foods, comprising three types of fatty acid — saturated, monounsaturated and polyunsaturated — in varying proportions. See also Monounsaturated fats; Polyunsaturated fats; Saturated fats.
Fibre: see Dietary fibre.
Filbert: see Hazelnut.
Frangelico: an Italian hazelnut liqueur.
Fromage frais: a soft smooth cheese made from skimmed milk. The *fromage frais* used in this book includes a small proportion of added cream and has an 8 per cent fat content.
Gelatine: a virtually tasteless protein, available in powdered form or in sheets. Dissolved gelatine is used to set mousses and fillings so that they retain their shape when unmoulded.
Ginger: the spicy, rootlike stem of the ginger plant, used dried and powdered as a flavouring. See also Preserved stem ginger.
Glacé fruit: fruit — usually cherries, peaches, pears, plums, figs, apricots or pineapple — preserved in sugar syrup, often used to decorate patisserie.
Glaze: to coat the surface of a tart or cake with a thin, shiny layer of melted jam or caramel.
Grand Marnier: a high-quality liqueur made from cognac and orange peel, which has a distinctive orange flavour.
Hazelnut: the fruit of a shrublike tree found primarily in Turkey, Italy and Spain, and in the United States. Filberts, which are cultivated, have a stronger flavour than hazelnuts, which grow wild. Both are prized by bakers and sweetmakers.
Icing sugar: finely ground granulated sugar, with a small amount of added cornflour to ensure a powdery consistency. Icing sugar's ability to dissolve instantly makes it ideal for glacé icings, where a grainy

texture is undesirable.
Jam without added sugar: jam which is sweetened by the sugar naturally found in fruit (fructose), rather than by added sugar (sucrose). Once opened it must be stored in the refrigerator, where it will keep for about three weeks.
Kataifi: a Greek pastry made in long thin strands like vermicelli. It can be bought ready made from continental delicatessens and speciality shops.
Kirsch (also called Kirschwasser): a clear cherry brandy distilled from small black cherries grown in Switzerland, Germany and the Alsace region of France.
Kiwi fruit: an egg-shaped fruit with a fuzzy brown skin, tart lime-green flesh and hundreds of tiny black edible seeds. Peeled and sliced horizontally, the kiwi displays a starburst of seeds at its centre that lends a decorative note to toppings.
Kumquat: a small, oval, orange fruit; both the skin and the flesh can be eaten.
Mango: a fruit grown throughout the tropics, with sweet, succulent, yellow-orange flesh that is extremely rich in vitamin A. It may cause an allergic reaction in some individuals.
Maple syrup: a sweet, golden syrup produced from the sap of the maple tree.
Marsala: a dark Sicilian dessert wine with a caramelized flavour.
Meringue: an airy concoction made from stiffly beaten egg whites and sugar. It can be baked to produce edible baskets, layered between sponge to make up a gateau, or served on its own.
Mixed candied peel: the peel of citrus fruit, soaked in a concentrated sugar solution. It can be bought whole, or already chopped.
Mixed spice: a mixture of ground spices that usually includes cinnamon, nutmeg and cloves and often also allspice, coriander and ginger. It should not be confused with mixed spices or pickling spices which are used in savoury dishes and include herbs and pepper as well.
Monounsaturated fats: one of the three types of fats found in foods. Monounsaturated fats are believed not to raise the level of cholesterol in the blood.
Muscovado sugar: originally, the name signified a brown sugar from the West Indian island of Barbados. Today the geographical connotation has gone, and the name is used for a mixture of unrefined sugar-cane juice and black treacle which is spun to produce a moist, dark brown sugar.
Orange-flower water: a liquid flavouring produced by distilling the oil extracted from the flowers of the bitter orange tree.
Parchment paper: a reusable paper treated with silicone to produce a non-stick surface. It is used to line tins and baking sheets.
Passion fruit: a juicy, fragrant, egg-shaped tropical fruit with wrinkled skin, yellow flesh and many small black seeds. The seeds are edible; the skin is not.
Pernod: an anise-flavoured spirit made in France.
Persimmon: a soft fruit with a deep orange flesh and skin.
Phyllo (also spelt "filo"): a paper thin flour and water

pastry popular in Greece and the Middle East. It can be made at home or bought, fresh or frozen, from delicatessens and shops specializing in Middle Eastern food. Because frozen phyllo dries out easily, it should be thawed in the refrigerator, and any phyllo sheets waiting to be filled should be covered with a damp towel.

Pine-nuts: seeds from the cones of the stone pine, a tree native to the Mediterranean. Toasting brings out their buttery flavour.

Pistachio nuts: prized for their pleasant flavour and green colour, pistachio nuts must be shelled and boiled for a few minutes before their skins can be removed.

Poach: to cook a food in barely simmering liquid. Fruit may be poached in water or a light syrup.

Polyunsaturated fats: one of the three types of fats found in foods. They exist in abundance in such vegetable oils as safflower, sunflower, corn and soya. Polyunsaturated fats lower the level of cholesterol in the blood.

Pomegranate: a red-skinned fruit with succulent edible seeds, which are picked out and eaten; the bitter white membranes are discarded. Pomegranates are in season in the autumn.

Poppy seeds: the spherical black seeds produced by a variety of poppy plant, and used as an ingredient in patisserie. Poppy seeds are so small that 500 g (1 lb) numbers nearly a million seeds.

Port: a ruby-coloured sweet dessert wine, originally from the Portuguese seaside town of Oporto, fortified with a small amount of brandy and usually aged in wooden casks.

Preserved stem ginger: pieces of peeled ginger root preserved in sugar syrup.

Purée: to reduce food to a smooth, even, pulplike consistency by mashing it, passing it through a sieve, or processing it in a food processor or a blender.

Quark: a type of soft cheese with a mild, clean, slightly acid flavour; usually very low in fat, but smoother varieties have added cream.

Quince: a small, hard, green or yellow-skinned fruit with a tart flavour. It cannot be eaten raw; the flesh turns pink when cooked.

Ramekin: a small, round, straight-sided glass or porcelain mould used to bake or serve a single portion of food.

Recommended Daily Amount (RDA): the average daily amount of an essential nutrient recommended for healthy people by the U.K. Department of Health and Social Security.

Reduce: to boil down a liquid in order to concentrate its flavour and thicken its consistency.

Ricotta: a soft, mild, white Italian cheese, made from cow's or sheep's milk. The low-fat ricotta used in this book has a fat content of about 8 per cent.

Rind: the flavourful outermost layer of citrus fruit peel; it should be cut or grated free of the white pith that lies beneath it.

Ring mould or savarin mould: a small circular mould with a hollow centre. Its open centre nearly doubles the food surfaces that are exposed to its walls, thus speeding up the cooking time.

Rose-water: a flavouring produced by distilling the oil of rose petals.

Safflower oil: a vegetable oil that contains the highest proportion of polyunsaturated fats.

Saffron: the dried reddish stigmas of the crocus flower, saffron yields a pungent flavour and a bright yellow colour. Powdered saffron may be substituted for the threads but has less flavour.

Saturated fats: one of the three types of fats found in foods. They exist in abundance in animal products and coconut and palm oils; they raise the level of cholesterol in the blood. Because high blood-cholesterol levels may cause heart disease, saturated fat consumption should be restricted to less than 15 per cent of the calories provided by the daily diet.

Savarin: a yeast-risen cake, soaked in sugar syrup and flavoured with a spirit such as rum or brandy. The cake is named after Brillat-Savarin, an 18th-century writer on gastronomical subjects.

Semolina: a coarse meal made from wheat.

Simmer: to maintain a liquid at a temperature just below its boiling point so that the liquid's surface barely ripples.

Skimmed milk: milk from which almost all the fat has been removed.

Sodium: a nutrient essential to maintaining the proper balance of fluids in the body. In most diets, a major source of the element is table salt, which contains 40 per cent sodium. Excess sodium may contribute to high blood pressure, which increases the risk of heart disease. One teaspoon (5.5 g) of salt, with 2,132 milligrams of sodium, contains just over the maximum daily amount recommended by the World Health Organization.

Streusel: a coarse crumb topping, usually made by combining flour, butter, sugar and flavourings.

Swiss roll tin: a shallow rectangular baking tin, about 2.5 cm (1 inch) deep.

Tia Maria: a coffee-flavoured liqueur from the Caribbean made using natural alcohol distilled from sugar cane.

Total fat: an individual's daily intake of polyunsaturated, monounsaturated and saturated fats. Nutritionists recommend that total fat constitute no more than 35 per cent of the energy in the diet. The term as used in this book refers to the combined fats in a given dish or food.

Vanilla extract: pure vanilla extract is the flavouring obtained by macerating vanilla pods in an alcohol solution. Artificial vanilla flavouring is chemically synthesized from clove oil.

Vanilla pod: the fermented and cured pod of a climbing orchid, native to Central America, used as a flavouring. The whole pod may be steeped in a liquid, or the pod may be split and the tiny black seeds inside scraped out and used.

Vanilla sugar: sugar flavoured by placing a whole vanilla pod in a closed container of sugar for at least a week.

Wholemeal flour: wheat flour which contains the whole of the wheat grain with nothing added or taken away. It is nutritionally valuable as a source of dietary fibre and is higher in B vitamins than white flour.

Yeast: a micro-organism which feeds on sugars and starches to produce carbon dioxide and thus leaven a cake or pastry. Yeast can be bought either fresh or dried; fresh yeast will keep for up to six weeks if stored in a refrigerator.

Yogurt: A smooth-textured, semi-solid cultured milk product. Low-fat yogurt contains about 1 per cent fat. Greek yogurt, which is made from full-cream milk, has a 10 per cent fat content.

Index

Picture Credits

Cover: Martin Brigdale. 4: top, James Murphy; bottom left, Graham Kirk; bottom right, Simon Butcher. 5: left and bottom, James Murphy; right, Chris Knaggs. 6: Chris Knaggs. 10-11: Andrew Whittuck. 12: top, Ian O'Leary; bottom, John Elliott. 13: John Elliott, except for bottom right by Ian O'Leary. 14-15: Chris Knaggs. 16: James Murphy. 17: John Elliott. 18: Chris Knaggs. 19: Graham Kirk. 20-21: Jan Baldwin. 22: Simon Butcher. 23: top, David Johnson; bottom, Chris Knaggs. 24: Martin Brigdale. 25: Graham Kirk. 26: Martin Brigdale. 27-28: Chris Knaggs. 29: top, Graham Kirk; bottom, John Elliott. 30: Chris Knaggs. 31: Graham Kirk. 32: Chris Knaggs. 33: Graham Kirk. 34: Chris Knaggs. 35: James Murphy. 36-38: Chris Knaggs. 39: James Murphy. 40: Chris Knaggs. 41: top, Chris Knaggs; bottom, Jan Baldwin. 42: Simon Butcher. 43: Jan Baldwin. 44-45: Martin Brigdale. 46: David Johnson. 47: James Murphy. 48: Chris Knaggs. 49: John Elliott. 50: James Murphy. 51: John Elliott. 52: Chris Knaggs. 53: Graham Kirk. 54: Simon Butcher. 55: Ian O'Leary. 56: Simon Butcher. 57: Chris Knaggs. 58: Graham Kirk. 59: John Elliott. 60: James Murphy. 61: Ian O'Leary. 62: Chris Knaggs. 63: James Murphy. 64-65: Chris Knaggs. 66: top, Graham Kirk; bottom, John Elliott. 67: Graham Kirk. 68-69: John Elliott. 70: top, Martin Brigdale; bottom, John Elliott. 71: John Elliott. 72: Jan Baldwin. 73: Simon Butcher. 74: James Murphy. 75-76: Graham Kirk. 77: Ian O'Leary. 78: Jan Baldwin. 79-80: James Murphy. 81: Martin Brigdale. 82: Simon Butcher. 83-85: James Murphy. 86: John Elliott. 87: top, John Elliott; bottom, Jan Baldwin. 88: Chris Knaggs. 89: Graham Kirk. 90: David Johnson. 91: John Elliott. 93: James Murphy. 94: John Elliott. 95-96: James Murphy. 97: Ian O'Leary. 98: John Elliott. 99: Ian O'Leary. 100-101: David Johnson. 102-103: Chris Knaggs. 104: James Murphy. 105-106: Jan Baldwin. 107: Chris Knaggs. 108: Martin Brigdale. 109: Simon Butcher. 110: Chris Knaggs. 111: David Johnson. 112: Chris Knaggs. 113: David Johnson. 114: Chris Knaggs. 115: Martin Brigdale. 116: Graham Kirk. 117: top, Martin Brigdale; bottom, John Elliott. 118: Jan Baldwin. 119: David Johnson. 120: Jan Baldwin. 121: Chris Knaggs. 122: top, Graham Kirk; bottom, John Elliott. 123: David Johnson. 124: Jan Baldwin. 125-126: Martin Brigdale. 127: James Murphy. 128: Martin Brigdale. 130: Chris Knaggs. 131: Simon Butcher. 132: Jan Baldwin. 133: Martin Brigdale. 134: John Elliott. 135: Chris Knaggs. 136-137: James Murphy.

Props: The Edtiors wish to thank the following outlets and manufacturers; all are based in London unless otherwise stated. 4: top: fork, Mappin & Webb Silversmiths; bottom left: marble, W.E. Grant & Co. (Marble) Ltd.; bottom right: napkins, Kilkenny; 5: left: china, Royal Worcester, Worcester; lace cloth, Laura Ashley Ltd.; 17: plates, Inshop; 19: china, Fortnum & Mason; 22: fork, Mappin & Webb Silversmiths; 23: bottom: pottery, Winchcombe Pottery, The Craftsmen Potters Shop; marble, W.E. Grant & Co. (Marble) Ltd.; 24: china, Fortnum & Mason; 27-28: china, Villeroy & Boch; 29: top: marble, W.E. Grant & Co. (Marble) Ltd.; 31: plate, The Conran Shop; 32: pottery, Kilkenny; 33: china, The Conran Shop; 34: china, Royal Worcester, Worcester; silver, Mappin & Webb Silversmiths; 37: marble, W.E. Grant & Co. (Marble) Ltd.; 38: plate, Hutschenreuther (U.K.) Ltd.; marble, W.E. Grant & Co. (Marble) Ltd.; 42: napkins, Kilkenny; 47: lace cloths, Laura Ashley Ltd.; 50: fork, Mappin & Webb Silversmiths; 52: plates, Royal Worcester, Worcester; 54: teaplate, cup and saucer, Chinacraft Ltd.; 55: china, Royal Worcester, Worcester; lace cloth, Laura Ashley Ltd.; 57: china, Hutschenreuther (U.K.) Ltd.; 58: platter, Hutschenreuther (U.K.) Ltd.; 59: plates, Royal Worcester, Worcester; forks, Mappin & Webb Silversmiths; 60: plate, A. & J. Young, The Craftsmen Potters Shop; 62: plate, Inshop; 64: marble, W.E. Grant & Co. (Marble) Ltd.; 66: top: plate, Fortnum & Mason; 67: plates, Villeroy & Boch; 68: plates, Villeroy & Boch; fork, Mappin & Webb Silversmiths; marble,

W.E. Grant & Co. (Marble) Ltd.; 69: plate, Royal Worcester, Worcester; marble, W.E. Grant & Co. (Marble) Ltd.; 70: plate, Hutschenreuther (U.K.) Ltd.; fork, Mappin & Webb Silversmiths; 71: china, The Conran Shop; 73: china, Villeroy & Boch; 75: plate, The Conran Shop; 76: china, Villeroy & Boch; 77: china, Hutschenreuther (U.K.) Ltd.; silver, Mappin & Webb Silversmiths; 78: plate, Chinacraft Ltd.; marble, W.E. Grant & Co. (Marble) Ltd.; 79: china, Chinacraft Ltd.; fork, Mappin & Webb Silversmiths; cake stand, Line of Scandinavia; 81: china, Hutschenreuther (U.K.) Ltd.; napkin, Kilkenny; 82: large plate, Rosenthal (London) Ltd.; 84: china, Royal Worcester, Worcester; lace cloth, Laura Ashley Ltd.; 85: plate, Spode, Worcester; 86: china, Hutschenreuther (U.K.) Ltd.; fork, Mappin & Webb Silversmiths; cloth, Ewart Liddell; 88: fork, Mappin & Webb Silversmiths; 89-90: marble, W.E. Grant & Co. (Marble) Ltd.; 91: plate, Hutschenreuther (U.K.) Ltd.; fork, Mappin & Webb Silversmiths; 94: plates, Inshop; 95: fork, Mappin & Webb Silversmiths; 97: china, Hutschenreuther (U.K.) Ltd.; marble, W.E. Grant & Co. (Marble) Ltd.; 98: china, Royal Worcester, Worcester; 100: marble, W.E. Grant & Co. (Marble) Ltd.; 101: china, Hutschenreuther (U.K.) Ltd.; 102-103, 109, 112: marble, W.E. Grant & Co. (Marble) Ltd.; 115: lace cloth, Laura Ashley; 116: plates, Rosenthal (London) Ltd.; 117: platter, Fortnum & Mason; teaplate, Royal Worcester, Worcester; 118: china, Hutschenreuther (U.K.) Ltd.; 120: plate, Royal Worcester; marble, W.E. Grant & Co. (Marble) Ltd.; 122: marble, W.E. Grant & Co. (Marble) Ltd.; 124: china, Hutschenreuther (U.K.) Ltd.; 125, 127: marble, W.E. Grant & Co. (Marble) Ltd.; 128: top plate, Hutschenreuther (U.K.) Ltd.; marble, W.E. Grant & Co. (Marble) Ltd.; 130: plate, Hutschenreuther (U.K.) Ltd.; 131: platter, Royal Worcester; marble, W.E. Grant & Co. (Marble) Ltd.; 132: plate, Hutschenreuther (U.K.) Ltd.; tablecloth, Ewart Liddell; 135: candlestick, Mappin & Webb Silversmiths: 136: marble, W.E. Grant & Co. (Marble) Ltd.; 137: china, Hutschenreuther (U.K.) Ltd.

Acknowledgements

The index for this book was prepared by Myra Clark. The editors also with to thank the following: Paul van Biene, London; René Bloom, London; Maureen Burrows, London; Alexandra Carlier, London; Windsor Chorlton, London; Eleanor Coleman, London; Jonathan Driver, London; Neil Fairbairn, Wivenhoe, Essex; Formica, Newcastle, Tyne and Wear; Tim Fraser, London; Wendy Gibbons, London; Irena Hoare, London; Molly Hodgson, Richmond, Yorkshire; Perstorp Warerite Ltd., London; Mario Pezzotta, London; Katherine Reeve, London; Sharp Electronics (U.K.) Ltd., London; Jane Stevenson, London; Miranda Tonbridge, London; Toshiba (U.K.) Ltd., London.

Colour separations by Fotolitomec, S.N.C., Milan, Italy
Typesetting by G. Beard & Son Ltd., Brighton, Sussex, England
Printed in Italy by New Interlitho S.p.A. - Milan